JAMES OGILVIE

Getting high

A world at my feet

Twinlaw

First Published in Great Britain 2015
by Twinlaw Publishing
Kirkcairn, Westruther, Gordon
Scottish Borders TD3 6NE

A CIP catalogue record for this title is available
from the British Library

Paperback ISBN: 978-0-9932220-0-9
Limited Edition Hardback ISBN 978-0-9932220-1-6

www.twinlawpublishing.co.uk

Rwenzori Summit

Contents

James Ogilvie

About the author

James' passion for wild places and 'getting high' stemmed from several family hill-walks in Wales and Scotland where he remembers surviving midges, rain and being dragged uphill in unsuitable footwear. Scouts and Duke of Edinburgh's Award camping trips followed and pretty soon it was off to Oxford University (Balliol College) and further-flung expeditions to places like Svalbard (see Chapter 1). An unlikely ascent of Kilimanjaro (Chapter 5) followed by Aconcagua (Chapter 6) seamlessly 'morphed' into his quest to climb the seven summits.

James' day time job has always been forestry. A Chartered Forester with a keen interest in trees, woods and forests, he has worked for the Forestry Commission for 35 years in many roles, including managing England's largest upland and lowland forests and overseeing grants and regulations in Scotland. He spent two years with the Lesotho woodlot project in southern Africa. Currently he heads up social & planning policy for Forestry Commission Scotland, managing a team of advisors dealing with planning, communities, access, recreation, health, learning and skills. As the owner of small woodland he knows the hands-on challenges - and priceless rewards - of looking after trees.

Rachel - to whom he was married for twenty years - bravely accompanied him to the backwoods of Canada (see Chapters 2-4) whilst Sarah – his partner for ten years – accompanied him up Kosciusko (see Chapter 11). He is immensely proud to be the father of Charles and Imogen and a father to James and Selina; all wonderful individuals who have brought him joy and inspiration.

James' other books include *Heritage Trees of Scotland* (a celebration of Scotland's amazing trees); *Staring Down on Stars* (an account of his Everest ascent); and *Adventure Holidays Worldwide* (dedicated to his late Uncle James who died in a climbing accident on the Matterhorn whilst an undergraduate at Balliol College).

After finishing the seven summits James is consoling himself by completing Scotland's Munros (282 mountains over 3,000ft high) with hill-loving friends. Only 40 to go now (but who's counting!).

This book is dedicated to –

Mum and Dad who always gave me a loving welcome home after each great escape.

Chhewang Nima Sherpa (c. 1967-2010) - my faithful Everest summit-day companion.

And all my **expedition buddies** over the years who put up with me with good grace.

Everest

Everest

Introduction - the Seven Summits

Everest

The Seven Summits - the highest mountains on each of the world's seven continents - are regarded by many as the crown jewels of mountaineering, a rare prize sought by many but attained by only a few. The number of Brits who have summited 'The Seven' is only around forty, whereas ten times that number have stood on top of Mt Everest; the most famous mountain in the world and of course Asia's highest point at 8,848m (29,029ft).

Similarly iconic is Kilimanjaro; at 5,963m (19,339ft) the highest point in Africa. Situated close to the equator in Tanzania, it still displays its majestic icecap, although its glacier -like so many others nowadays - is shrinking due to the effects of global warming. At 6,196m (20,320ft) North America's highest mountain - Mt McKinley or Denali as it is usually called today - is better known than its South American counterpart - Aconcagua 6,962m (22,840ft). Denali lies far north in Alaska, its harsh weather and crevassed environment a good testing ground for would-be Everest climbers. By contrast, Aconcagua in Argentina has been called 'the highest hill-walk in the world'. Though non-technical, it still offers a demanding challenge as the highest mountain outside the Himalayas and one beset by challenging weather.

Although Mt Blanc is the highest mountain in political Europe, it is Mt Elbrus 5,633m (18,481ft) in the Russian Caucasus range that takes the prize as the highest point in geographic Europe. Mt Vinson 4,897m (16,067ft) is the highest point in Antarctica. Finally, opinions are divided about whether Australia or Oceania is counted as being the seventh continent, but 'down under' there lies a lowly but transcendent peak - Mt Kosciuszko 2,228m (7,310ft) - the highest in Australia.

Each of the seven summits is unique, each special in its own way. Each varies in its technical demands and each provides an excuse - as if any were needed - for climbing amongst the most spectacular scenery in the world. At one level, climbing the Seven could be thought of as a self-centred ego trip, a kind of glorified 'Munro bagging' on a global scale. Therefore, partly to assuage my conscience but mainly because I believe that Tree Aid performs vitally important work, I have raised some £50,000 for that charity through all my climbs to date. "*And what then?*" you may ask. "*What does a chap do after summiting the Seven?*" Well, it's a little known fact that the 2nd highest summits in the world's continents are more technically demanding than the highest. Now THERE'S a challenge...

Admit that once you have got up
from your chair and opened the door,
once you have walked out into the clean air
toward that edge and taken the path up high
beyond the ordinary, you have become
the privileged and the pilgrim,
the one who will tell the story
and the one, coming back
from the mountain,
who helped to make it.

From **Mameen** by **David Whyte** (printed with permission from
Many Rivers Press www.davidwhyte.com)

And they sing as they march with their flags unfurled
Today in the mountains, tomorrow the world.

From **Brothers in Arms** (printed with permission from **Dire Straits**)

Everest

Seven Summits Foreword – Stephen Venables

James and I share a great grandfather, William Maxwell Ogilvie, who was, briefly, a mountaineer. In the summer of 1872, just short of his twentieth birthday, he made several alpine climbs around Zermatt, including what must have been a very early ascent of the Weisshorn. He wanted desperately to climb the Matterhorn, but his mother, mindful of the terrible accident on the first ascent seven years earlier, forbade it, and the mountain became known in the Ogilvie family as the Mutterhorn.

So there is mountaineering in our blood. Over a century after our great grandfather's alpine excursions, James and I spent a year sharing a condemned house at the far end of Oxford's Woodstock Road. It was very Gothic and we called it Gormenghastly. I can remember Matt Ridley coming round for supper one evening and showing slides of his and James' recent Svalbard expedition. The expedition's ostensible purpose, as James explains in the opening chapter of this book, was the ornithological study of some arctic waders called grey phalaropes; its real purpose was to go on a great adventure.

James has managed to continue going on great adventures, most recently flying to the heart of the Antarctic continent to climb the last of his seven continental summits, Vinson. Since Dick Bass and Pat Morrow become the first people to reach all the continental tops during the eighties, the 'Seven Summits' has become an increasingly popular modern phenomenon. So for me much of the charm of this book lies in James' other journeys to more esoteric mountains, such as the trek to Mt Brown, in the Canadian Rockies, following in the steps of that great Scottish plant collector William Douglas, or his ascent of Margherita, named in 1906 after the Duke of Abruzzi's aunt when the Duke became the first to reach this highest point of the weird and wonderful Rwenzori mountains on the cloud enshrouded border of Uganda and Congo.

In his account of climbing Margherita in 2003, James mentions how it took an hour to scramble over rocks from the the hut to the start of the Elena Glacier. When I was there in

1987 we were on the ice ten minutes after leaving the hut. And that was nothing to do with our fitness – no-one runs at 4,500 metres – just a graphic reminder of how fast the world's glaciers are shrinking. In the case of these equatorial mountains, there may soon be no ice left at all. I just hope that the magnificent forests will remain. Which brings me to another thing we have in common – a love of trees. In my case the enthusiasm is entirely amateur, with James it is the dendrological dedication of a professional who has spent his whole working life with the Forestry Commission. And still managed to sneak off and climb the Seven Summits! And, in the process, raise money for the important charity Tree Aid.

Reaching the top of every continent requires a lot of determination. Unless you happen to have a large private income, the greatest challenge is probably getting leave from work and raising the considerable funds – particularly for the very expensive charter flight to Antarctica. You also have to be very fit. And in the case of the highest mountain of all you do have to stick your neck out and accept a certain level of risk. James embraced that risk and got his reward, and I like to think that William Ogilvie would be pleased to know that two of his great grandchildren have now stood on the summit of Mount Everest.

Stephen Venables
March 2015

Mount Vinson

Charles Ogilvie

Preface – Charles Ogilvie

It all started with my Great Great Grandfather William M. Ogilvie. Actually, you could probably trace its origins back to the very beginnings of Clan Ogilvie and the epics of Scottish history, even going back to Robert the Bruce, if our somewhat fanciful family tree is to be believed. Wherever it began, the spirit of restless adventure seems to be part of the Ogilvie DNA. It was carried on by my Grandfather, David Ogilvie: in his youth, he cycled from Rugby to Jedburgh, a distance of more than two hundred and fifty miles, on a three-geared bicycle.

And the spirit of adventure lives on in my father James, whose love of the world's mountains and wild places is well documented in these pages. I still look back fondly on adventures we've shared, in the Lake District, Scotland, Canada, Turkey, Egypt. Indeed, one of my earliest memories is of a spending a worried night on shore with my mum and sister, while Dad was out on a boat in the raging storm. The worry was bad enough for my six-year-old self; I can only imagine what my poor mother went through. Fortunately the boat and its crew had managed to put ashore on an island for the night and returned safely, if somewhat bedraggled, the next morning. I don't think it's a coincidence that since then Dad's shown more of an affinity for the mountains than the sea!

The seven summits is a remarkable feat, and there's lots to celebrate. But there's one family member who I think would be particularly proud of my father. James William Ogilvie, my Great-Uncle, was another restless spirit. Some of his youthful letters survive, and the vivid details of his travels spring from the page as if he were speaking to you over a 'cuppie' – his favourite pick-me-up after a long day. His time in the Army in World War II, France, Holland, and afterwards India and Burma; rambles in the English countryside during army training… the scenes and characters speak of James' thoughtful and observant mind, and they live on because of his determination to set it all down in writing.

One of the most memorable letters tells of a Scottish climbing expedition during his university holidays in 1948, with wind and snowstorms, hard bunks and leaky roofs; carving steps up the snowy hillside and glissading down; frozen clothes and sodden boots; the chill of cold nights and the joy of resting tired limbs and enjoying a warm dinner after a long day on the hills; the surprise at startling a herd of deer or a waddling ptarmigan, and through it all, the beauty of Scotland's '*patchwork of browns and blues and dark greens*' or the '*gleam of the snow-slopes drenched by the moonlight*'. At least, all this when the changeable Scottish weather allowed him to see anything!

This expedition was a trial for Great Uncle James' attempt on the Matterhorn in Switzerland during the summer of the same year. Tragically he and his friends fell, roped together, on their descent and were all killed. They are buried in the English cemetery in Zermatt. Had his life not been cut short, who knows what other adventures James and his friends might have had. Perhaps they would have further inspired my Dad.

This happened before my father was born, so James senior never met James junior. But I can't help thinking that had he lived, he might have approved of these adventures and the way they've been committed to writing.

Sonnet
Death is no enemy to those who seek
And scale the mountain-tops of life and time,
To meet their end upon some mighty peak
Of man's experience, ruthless and sublime.
Yet not their end; for who that sees this place
Can doubt the Maker's pattern, shade and sun,
Defeat redeemed by victory, triumphs won
Which light the blazing glory of His Face?

And how should we forget thee, undismayed
By years of peril, whose untarnished soul
Soared free to find its own allotted goal;
Leaving the mortal man, his ransom paid,
To sleep serene amid the snows untrod
Where dwells the awful Majesty of God?

Vera Brittain

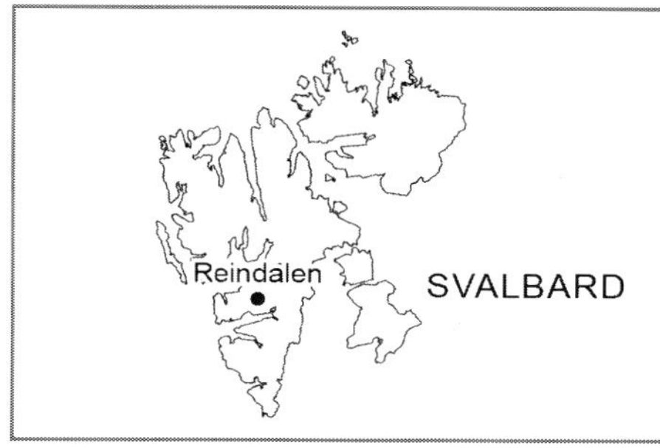

1

An Arctic adventure –

Oxford University Svalbard expedition (1978)

My first 'proper' expedition, involving lots of enthusiasm but little experience, set off for polar bear country just a few hundred miles from the North Pole…

"*Even though polar bears are unusual in your study area during the summer,*" the Sysselmann's letter read, "*expeditions to Svalbard are advised to take a weapon in self-defence.*"

The Oxford University 1978 expedition to Svalbard would be no exception. Matt's .303 rifle was pressed into service along with twenty rounds of anti-bear ammunition, the latter neatly packed in a sealed box to satisfy customs regulations. At Heathrow airport they took this firearm very seriously. A security guard was assigned to our four-man party, ushering us through customs and only leaving our side when the rifle was safely stowed aboard the aeroplane. By contrast, Oslo airport's security was relaxed. After the first of the three flights from Britain to Svalbard, the lethal weapon emerged - unaccompanied and unnoticed by us - onto the luggage carousel. It was some time before we realised that both weapon and ammunition were waiting for us, still unguarded, at the end of the conveyor belt, along with other unclaimed luggage.

After a six hour wait we boarded the next aircraft, a Scandinavian Airlines System DC-9 with the unlikely name of 'Burnt Viking'. "*Why on earth,*" we wondered, "*would a Viking be burnt? Surely it was a Viking's job to do the burning?*" We were still pondering this mystery when Burnt Viking took off over the idyllic lakes and fjords of southern Norway. As we headed ever northwards, dark green blankets of conifer forests gradually gave way to sparse dwarf scrub as the Arctic Circle slipped invisibly past us twenty five thousand feet below.

If Oslo's security appeared less than strict, Tromsø's was positively blasé. We made our way into the baggage claim area to find the rifle casually piled onto an airport trolley, along with the rest of our kit. Settling down to wait for the last of our three flights, we revelled in the novelty of the midnight sun. "*Might as well get used to it,*" we agreed, basking outside the terminal building.

From now on we would not see proper darkness for several weeks.

No loudspeakers announced flight SK380 to Svalbard, due to depart at 00.50. Instead, a general consensus of opinion replaced the 'boarding now' formalities of larger airports and a handful of waiting passengers shuffled towards the exit barrier and the waiting DC-9 ('Bent Viking' this time – "*Some sort of Scandinavian Quasimodo? A gay warrior? Both, perhaps?*"). Once more we mused over the oddities of aircraft nomenclature as the DC-9 taxied for take-off. Rising above the stunted birch and willow trees lining the runway, we realised that the vegetation surrounding us in Svalbard would be miniscule by comparison. As we headed towards the North Pole, the 'Paris of the North' slipped swiftly behind us, leaving only the blue emptiness of the Barents Sea.

Five hundred miles of water separates Spitsbergen - the largest island in the Svalbard archipelago - from north Norway. Scandinavians are thought to have discovered Svalbard some eight hundred years ago. Traditional Norse stories tell of a land known as Svalbarð (literally 'cold shores'). For centuries the islands were used by the Norwegians, Dutch, English, Danish, French and Russians for whaling and for hunting walrus, fox and polar bear. International tensions continued until 1920 when the Spitsbergen Treaty granted full sovereignty to Norway, recognising Svalbard as a free economic and demilitarised zone and granting non-discriminatory rights to signatory countries for fishing, hunting and mineral resources. Today, Svalbard's Norwegian sovereignty is guarded by a Governor – the Sysselmann – who has powers of jurisdiction, policing and administration over the islands.

Our first glimpse of Svalbard from the air revealed a cluster of nunataks, winding glaciers and ice-bound fjords contrasting with patches of darker tundra. Minutes later the plane started its descent towards Longyearbyen runway. Opened only three years previously by King Olaf V, this airfield has made a huge difference to arriving expeditions. Before then, travel to Spitsbergen was only possible by boat and therefore confined to the summer months when the fjords are relatively ice-free. Somewhat bizarrely in this land of ice and snow, the runway is painted white, although it makes sense when you realise that it's in order to reflect the sun's rays and avoid melting the permafrost beneath. Even more bizarre however, is the presence of coal mines and conveyor gantries, visible proof of Svalbard's dominant commercial activity since the early 20th century. Below the backdrop of these hillside mineshafts, rows of mineworker chalets, straggling on their stilt foundations, comprised the island's main settlement. Construction work was evident: during our 1978 summer expedition so many new buildings sprang up at the island's main settlement that the place appeared visibly different by the end of the season.

And so at 2.30 in the morning four travel-weary explorers stepped out of the cosseted comfort of the aircraft and into the chilly wind sweeping Longyearbyen airfield; the Oxford University 1978 expedition to Svalbard had arrived at last! But before being allowed to camp we had to undergo the necessary formalities, including proof of self-sufficiency in food supplies. This required some explanation, since the bulk of our equipment was due to arrive shortly by boat. There are a few stores in Longyearbyen but they cater only for local inhabitants. This explains why visitors arriving without food at Svalbard's main settlement are likely to be bundled unceremoniously onto the next homeward bound plane.

The rifle we had regarded as a mixed blessing: a nuisance to carry and extra weight as well. As the Governor of Svalbard's letter had pointed out, polar bears are usually very scarce in the west of Svalbard during the summer since the main population is to be found at Nordaustland and Kong Karl's land, over two hundred miles away. For a bear to be seen near the island's main settlement is rare indeed. It was thus with utter disbelief that the expedition awoke the next morning to the sound of a car engine revving outside the tent, its driver frantically shouting "*Isbjorn, isbjorn!*" (Ice bear) and pointing to where, not one hundred yards away, the yellow-white outline of a polar bear could be seen shuffling along. This information sparked a frantic scuffle inside the tent while a desperate search was made… not for the .303 rifle, but for a camera with a telephoto lens, as the receding bear shape disappeared into the distance.

Our temporary campsite near the airfield was shared with an Italian expedition, not one of whom spoke English, which necessitated conversing in rather broken French. We learned that the purpose of their expedition was to commemorate with a plaque the ill-fated attempt by the Italian general Umberto Nobile, to cross the Polar ice cap by airship. The extraordinary account of this ill-fated fiasco is worth a brief mention here: Designed by Nobile, the 'Italia' airship did reach the Pole on May 24th 1928 but a day later it crashed onto pack ice in a storm some thirtykilometers north of Svalbard. Of the sixteen crew, ten were thrown onto the ice while the rest were trapped in the gondola as it swept skyward following impact. Although the airship may later have exploded, both it - and its six remaining crew - were never seen again. After the alarm was eventually raised, several nations launched the first recorded polar air and sea rescue effort. Even Nobile's competitor - Roald Amundsen (who pipped Scott to the South Pole in 1911) - set aside past differences and boarded a French seaplane heading for the rescue headquarters. Tragically this plane also disappeared and Amundsen's body was never found. After a month of privation for the Italia survivors, the first rescue plane managed to land near the Italia crash site. Nobile was airlifted successfully but when the plane returned to pick up the other survivors it too crash landed. Talked about a jinxed adventure! Eventually, after enduring forty eight days on the ice floe, the last of Nobile's surviving crew were rescued by a Soviet icebreaker.

The purpose of our expedition was more prosaic but more scientifically rewarding, for we were there to research the behaviour of the grey phalarope (*Phalaropus fulicarius*) a small migratory wader with a curious reversed sex role…but more of that anon. Our main preoccupation at this stage was to complete arrangements for reaching our final destination: the Stormyrvatna (Great Marsh Lakes) an area of wetland near the mouth of the Reindalen (reindeer valley) some thirty miles south of Longyearbyen. Our first task was to collect the remaining supplies which - to our undisguised relief - arrived as scheduled on the Tromsø mail steamer, along with - bizarrely - several deep freezers (the expression 'selling freezers to the Eskimo' will never seem the same again). As this was the first boat of the season to arrive, it was greeted with much enthusiasm by the islanders gathered at the dockside. There was even a brass band adding to the festive atmosphere as the vessel edged its way slowly towards the quayside.

Reunited with our kit, we now had to solve the problem of how to get the stuff to our expedition base at Reindalen. Frozen fjords prohibited using boats to ferry the equipment, whilst carrying supplies through the snow-covered mountains would have taken us precious weeks. So we decided to split into two groups: Matt accompanying the bulk of the stores by helicopter; Dave, Charles and I chartering a Cessna to Sveagruva - a small mining settlement some twenty miles east of the camp - and then trekking along Van Mijen Fjord to rejoin Matt. After loading Matt's white and orange chopper to capacity we discovered that its pilot rejoiced in the name of 'Joking' (hard to resist the temptation to exclaim "*You must be joking!*" to every remark he made). However, the last laugh was on him, for it was only after the chopper had swept around in an arc and disappeared towards the south that we discovered that one of our sizeable food packages - a twelve man-day ration - had been overlooked. The thought of carrying all that extra weight left us rather despondent until we hit on the simple but brilliant idea of chucking it out of the plane near the camp, en route to 'Svea'. We worried that this brainwave might be dismissed by our Cessna pilot, but we were quite wrong. Ingrid Pederson turned out to be a glamorous blond Norwegian quite unfazed by the would-be derring-do of young Oxford undergraduates. No stranger to Polar travel herself, she had over twenty five years flying experience, including having once crossed from Canada to Norway via the North Pole. A mere air-drop was simply 'business as usual' to her.

But not to us however. It was with some misgivings that we finalised our hasty plans for 'Operation Airdrop'. As the ground fell away below we were able to form a good impression of the conditions we would encounter later on. Not for nothing does Spitsbergen translate as 'land of the pointy mountains'. Nestling high in the network of 3,000 foot peaks lay glaciers, dazzling white in the clear air, while the lower slopes supported a mantle of pristine snow broken only by the occasional marks of skidoo tracks. For the most part the terrain consisted of beautiful unbroken wilderness stretching as far as the eye could see. Not surprisingly therefore, it took several minutes of searching before the camp was sighted not far from a solitary unoccupied hut. These remote 'hytte' are a feature of Svalbard's valleys, being accessible to skidoos in winter and inflatable boats in summer. About half are privately owned, used for hunting trips, whilst the rest are owned by SNSK. Sometimes abbreviated simply to 'Store Norske', the Store Norske Spitsbergen Kulkompani is a Norwegian coal mining company formed in 1916.

As we circled around the hut a couple of times, Matt waved up at us from below. We opened the door wide, waiting for the right moment and then - under Ingrid's command - we launched forth the air-to-ground food package. As an airborne manoeuvre it was an unqualified success. As a parcel delivery it was an unmitigated disaster. Food containers of every conceivable type disintegrated spectacularly upon impact with the hard permafrost, spewing their contents over a considerable area of tundra that smelt curiously of curry powder for some considerable time afterwards. Matt gamely scooped up the remains of digestive biscuits, dehydrated savoury meals and custard powder as best he could. This mixture we later came to know well - rather too well in fact. We christened it 'Sproggits' - but that didn't make it taste any better.

Some twenty minutes and many photographs later we were deposited by Ingrid at Sveagruva on what might optimistically be described as an airstrip but which actually consisted of an uneven and rattling expanse of stones and pebbles. As we shouldered our rucksacks we waved goodbye to Ingrid and set off along Van Mijen Fjord. After two days marching we rounded a corner and gazed at the place we had all travelled so far to see. Before us lay three orange tents, one for stores and the other two our home for the next five weeks. Close by stood a flock of barnacle geese standing to attention with heads held erect, like a group of emissaries sent to welcome us to Stormyrvatna.

This corner of Svalbard had been chosen as our expedition base for several reasons. The pools and marshes close to the camp formed ideal habitat for nesting and breeding birds. Although ornithological study of the grey phalarope was the main raison d'être of the expedition, we were also interested in researching the other local birdlife, including purple sandpipers, and the less common arctic terns, golden plovers, king and common eiders, long-tailed ducks, arctic skuas and red-throated divers. Above the valley's wetlands mountainous scree slopes formed suitable habitat for snow buntings, whilst above them amongst the cliffs nested barnacle geese.

As might by gathered by its name, Reindalen was also home to many reindeer (on one occasion we counted two hundred and twenty) and part of our research project was to investigate the ecosystem nitrogen cycle, from deer droppings to decomposition and eventual nutrient release. The reunion of our four-man team heralded much rejoicing, followed by a recce of the Stormyrvatna terrain. We set about compiling a detailed map of the area, and - under a long and noble OU expedition tradition - started ascribing names to features such as the lakes. Whilst we realised that our efforts would be ephemeral, there exist some more permanent names on the map of Svalbard – names that remain to this day, including Oxfordbreen (Oxford glacier), Isis Point and Balliolbreen, for example.

The grey phalarope was chosen as the main research objective of our expedition for several reasons. This species is unusually tame and approachable. During courtship displays they are almost completely oblivious of other creatures - including humans - and except when they are with chicks, it's generally possible to approach within a few metres, greatly assisting observation. Distinguishing the sexes is easy: the female is larger than the male (roughly the size of a thrush) and is more brightly coloured. The females pursue males, compete for nesting territory, and defend their nests and chosen mates aggressively. Soon after the females lay their olive-brown eggs, they begin their southward migration, leaving the males to incubate the eggs and care for the young. Chicks develop rapidly, being able to fly within eighteen days of birth. Phalaropes are presented with a unique problem at egg laying: the female must ensure that her mate knows where she has laid the eggs whilst the male needs some assurance that the eggs he will incubate are those that he fathered. We wanted to know how they solved that problem and we were interested in their behaviour before and after egg-laying, so that we could test some predictions as to why the female deserts her mate.

Our arctic existence soon settled down to a daily routine. After breakfast we each set out towards different locations, armed with field glasses, notebooks and stopwatches. The latter helped precision in studying the feeding requirements of males and females in different situations and at different stages of the breeding season. A small dictating machine was used to record observations. This proved particularly useful during our phalarope studies since it was often difficult to keep pace with a succession of different behavioural activities whilst trying to write with numb fingers. Because the breeding terrain was spread out, we usually took lunch with us and stayed out all 'day'. Dinner was timed by watches rather than hunger pangs: without a strict routine in the 24 hour daylight, we would probably have finished our food supplies all too soon! The midnight sun held a love-hate relationship for us. Although it avoided the need for torches, allowing us to read, write or work at any time, we found that sleeping was difficult – that is until we became accustomed to the 'lights being left on'.

Within a few days we were able to predict where phalarope pairs would be found and could recognise new arrivals. Later on, when all the nests in the area had been pinpointed and a daily check kept on the varying stages of incubation, the work became slightly easier. But to start with a mass of courtship behavioural data had to be collected. After some days we came to know the egg-laying ceremony well and we soon became familiar with the distinguishing marks of certain birds, especially males. Eventually we were even able to detect individual idiosyncrasies. One male phalarope in particular was so tame that he could be stroked on the nest. For obvious reasons 'Strokey' became a favourite of ours.

During the next few weeks the local lake ice retreated as the arctic summer advanced, revealing an ever-growing carpet of lush green tundra. This consisted mainly of moss with a diminutive forest of heel-high arctic willow (Salix polaris) whilst in the wetter areas, cotton grass and rushes abounded. These species formed the staple diet of the local reindeer herd. Occasional tufts of coarse white hair would contrast with the darker tundra, indicating that the reindeer were molting into their brown and grey summer coats. Clearly unused to humans, these short-sighted animals would often approach inquisitively, circling downwind to get a better sense of what they were dealing with, their large liquid brown eyes searching for any sign of hostility. Then scenting a no-doubt pungent whiff of Oxford undergraduate they would throw back their heads and disappear at a fast trot, hind legs splayed out like some disjointed fantoccini. Two young reindeer in particular became relatively tame, often hanging around our camp. We called them Bill and Ben. One day I was observing Bill when, out of the corner of my eye, I became aware of Ben getting closer and closer. His muzzle stretched towards my face and his hot breath condensed on my glasses, obscuring my vision. Although I couldn't see what happened next there was no mistaking it - my beard was being chewed tentatively. Very soon Ben realised that this was not the tasty clump of tundra that he had anticipated and made off at full speed, no doubt highly embarrassed by his mistake. My reaction was more of amusement than anything else - after all it's not everyone who can say they've been nibbled by a reindeer. But as their coats changed from winter to summer colour, Bill, Ben and the other reindeer became much more shy, particularly the females with their (usually single) offspring.

The repeated freezing and thawing that is prevalent in Svalbard can have significant effects upon rock weathering and geomorphology. When water freezes its volume increases by nearly a tenth and this expansion can displace or fracture rocks. Thus we were sometimes woken by a mini avalanche of dislodged rocks falling from the cliffs half a mile east of our camp. Frost formation can heave soil above the permafrost, making it futile to try and bury any rubbish. The 'Environmental Regulations for Spitsbergen' booklet given to all visiting expeditions advised either burning rubbish or burying it in a scree. Not all visitors were as fastidious however, as the presence of old cans and bottles testified around the hut not far from our camp. But occasionally the frost turned up something interesting, like the bird ring I picked up a mile from the camp. After returning to Britain I duly obliged the 'Urgent – return Stavanger Museum' instruction printed on the ring and several days later back came the reply that ring number 205 118 had been placed on an adult Pink-footed goose in Reindalen by a Mr Russel Webbe on 14 July 1954. Being little worn, the ring can only have been carried for a year or two, remaining unburied by the permafrost's action and conspicuous in the short tundra vegetation.

One of the oddities of freeze-thaw action is the arctic Pingo. Roughly translated from the Eskimo language as 'isolated hill' these features comprise large conical mounds forced upwards by an expanding core of ice which remains frozen even in summer. This fact has been exploited in the past by Arctic peoples who used them to store food in the summer (this practice clearly now being replaced by deep freezers - as evidenced by the supply boat). Five of the Svalbard's best Pingos were reported to exist in upper Reindalen, rising abruptly from the tundra and appearing like mini volcanoes. This prompted Dave and me to undertake a small expedition up the valley in search of this unusual phenomenon. Unfortunately our trek coincided with a sharp thaw which made crossing the glacial melt water somewhat nerve-wracking and requiring a tactical approach via the wider braids and flatter stretches. Not far from the nearest Pingo we chanced upon a beautiful ice cave, its entrance formed from a collapsed ice sheet roof. In retrospect we should probably have thought twice before entering this potentially perilous structure but we were intrigued by the beautiful blues and greens shining through its translucent ice dome. Happily we emerged unscathed some time later. In the end we visited three Pingos. Each one held a particular fascination, at one a display of diverse wild flowers, at the next a collection of reindeer bones and at the last, the presence of an Arctic fox lair whence emanated the high-pitched yelping of hungry cubs. The vixen arrived soon afterwards, withdrew to a respectful distance and sat on her haunches observing us and scratching her part-winter, part-summer fur coat.

Half-way through our expedition the normally benign weather decided to show us a thing or two and a full-blown arctic gale whipped up out of nowhere, threatening to blow our Vango Force 10 tents away. When the winds did eventually subside we discovered that we had a new visitor - a sedge warbler. The poor bird had been blown hundreds of miles outside its range. Any warbler in Svalbard is a curiosity since even the arctic warbler - the most northerly distributed of all the warblers - is confined to the north of Norway. This hapless visitor was clearly disorientated and confused by the lack of bushy vegetation. It had to make do with sheltering in old tin cans littering the hut area, playing hide and seek with us as we tried to photograph it. After a few days he flew off - we know not where - and never returned, although we like to think that he made it back to Norway. Another avian visitor was less fortunate however. A glaucus gull decided to make our camp his camp and as the days passed he grew more and more tame. However, it transpired that this was because he was becoming less and less well. Several days later, instead of flying off when we approached, it remained on the ground, its head drooping pathetically. We tried to keep it warm and administered some fish but it continued its inexorable terminal decline…

Other birds were not so shy or so sick. An arctic skua made its nest half a mile from our camp, dive-bombing us if we approached too closely. More than one reindeer straying into this aggressive bird's territory became the object of aerial coat clawing. Arctic terns too would screech at intruders and unceremoniously dive bomb them. More secretive were the red-throated divers that merged cryptically into the background of their island nests, and the purple sandpipers that would remain motionless on their clutch, only leaving the nest at the last possible moment. Then they would put on a convincing distraction display, running along the ground and drooping their wings, pathetically trying to sidetrack intruders away from the nest.

Some miles south east of the camp in Littledalen, lay a secluded gorge, carved out of the rock by a rushing torrent. An abundance and diversity of flowers below the cliff ledges revealed a nitrogen-rich environment - the result of many years of goose guano, for this was a perfect nesting spot for barnacle geese. These proud birds would sit patiently while we surreptitiously edged - commando style - towards them, cameras poised to capture their jet black necks and sleek grey and white bodies. This place was also home to an arctic fox vixen and her cubs, as we were soon to discover. Charles became so absorbed in taking photographs that he failed to see the vixen boldly approaching him from behind. She promptly seized his hat and trotted proudly off with it. Not content with merely thieving, she then proceeded to leave her calling card, thoroughly drenching the offending article in pungent fox pee and then scampering off defiantly. The odour defied Charles' most determined attempts to remove it and for a long time afterwards we insisted on the smelly hat being quarantined.

By this stage in the expedition we had pinpointed all fifteen phalarope nests in Stormyrvatna.

A lack of ground features meant that we had to be careful about marking their whereabouts: if we had used marker flags the cunning little vixen would have quickly established that flag equals food. Eventually we hit upon the idea of using cast antlers left behind by the reindeer herd, and taking compass bearings from these markers. In practice this worked well.

As the days passed, Van Mijen fjord turned from white to blue. This is the point in Svalbard's summer when there is a real danger of Polar Bear attack. After a sudden ice thaw bears can sometimes become stranded, unable to follow the floes northward. Deprived of their normal diet of seals they can become threatening and potentially dangerous. We made sure the rifle was to hand. Throughout all this time, without radio or other communications, we were completely oblivious to news of the outside world, isolated from other humans apart from the occasional drone of a helicopter or Ingrid's Cessna. The four of us had become surprisingly well adapted to this isolation, taking only each other's existence for granted. Therefore, when Matt suddenly exclaimed "*homo sapiens!*" as we were finishing supper one evening, at first no one of us believed him, that is, until a wild looking Norwegian with a rifle slung over his back and pulled along by two husky dogs, appeared in camp. It turned out that he had not spoken to another human being for several weeks so he was glad to converse with us in broken English over a mug of cocoa. An employee of Store Norske, he was on his way back to Longyearbyen after spending three months in the south, staying in huts and living on seal meat. 'Norske' as we later nicknamed him, had some amazing stories to tell, not least his recent attack by a polar bear which killed one of his dogs (worth £200 in 1978). Listening to his stories we were glad that we had decided to bring the .303 after all. We parted on the best of terms. 'Norske' whistled his dogs, gave a friendly farewell and disappeared as abruptly as he had arrived.

The end of June brought more gale force winds. For three days we were grounded and we even had to abandon our tents and make for the security of the hut. Mercifully, little damage was sustained: some buckled tent poles and a few objects thrown about. However, the whereabouts of a solid wooden crate lid marked 'Oxford University Expedition to Svalbard 1978' still remains a mystery. We searched high and low but it must have been blown for miles. If anyone finds it will they please let me know?

At about this time we received another visit from the outside world. A distant roar of helicopter blades could be heard and we prepared to wave as in the past. But instead of flying overhead, the Jet Ranger started to descend. We hastily set about gathering vulnerable equipment and waited to greet the tall fair haired man who stepped down onto the tundra. After shaking our hands he informed us that he was the local police chief and produced some paperwork from his pocket –

happily not an official summons, but some very welcome mail from home. He kindly agreed to take our equipment back to Longyearbyen and we thanked him as we waved him off.

During early July arctic foxes and skuas had taken their toll of phalarope young. The chicks that had survived predation could be seen picking their way through the sparse undergrowth whilst the male remained nearby, calling to them from time to time. Females who had not yet managed to secure a mate - or another mate - started to form loose flocks in preparation for their long migration south. By mid-July, phalarope activity had declined significantly. Most of the adults had flown south on the start of their five thousand mile migration to the southern hemisphere. Our main research work was nearly over. It was time to start the return to civilisation some thirty miles distant. Although we were sorry to be leaving the area we had called home for five weeks, the absence of phalaropes now gave Stormyrvatna a rather lifeless atmosphere. A powdering of newly fallen snow on the surrounding mountain tops gave a foretaste of the end of summer: yes, it was time to be leaving…

Although we had much less to carry than at the start of the expedition, it was still necessary to make depots and leap-frog back and forth, covering the distance from our camp back to Longyearbyen three times over. The route up Reindalen and Gangdalen required several river crossings through thigh-level ice-cold melt water. Snow-clad mountains and screes, fast-flowing streams and rocky outcrops made the place look uncannily like a Scottish Glen and a poignant reminder of home. After much effort we eventually reached the Tillbergfonna, a network of glaciers surrounding the Gangskardet watershed and the start of our trek down Todalen towards civilisation.

When we did reach Longyearbyen the place was unrecognisable. What had been ours and the Italians' exclusive campsite now resembled an international congress, with flags of many countries fluttering from twenty or more tents. New buildings had sprung up, the coal-bearing conveyor belts were rattling in their gantries, and distant cars resembled strange garish toys. After five weeks virtually to ourselves it was difficult adjusting to the presence of so many people. Part of us was missing the wilds of Stormyrvatna already. Clearly this arctic experience had changed each one of us in subtle but enduring ways.

Just before we departed we saw something that made us smile: a poster warning of the dangers of polar bear attacks. The Oxford University 1978 expedition to Svalbard expedition had had one close encounter of a bear kind at the start and one vicarious encounter via Norske in the middle. There would be no more. The rifle and rounds remained unfired and that was good enough for us.

The other members of the 1978 Oxford University expedition to Svalbard comprised Charles Gillow, Dave Perkins and Matt Ridley. Matt read zoology at Magdalen; Dave read geography at St Catherine's; and Charles and I read agricultural and forest science: Charles at Keeble, myself at Balliol. Although we never did another expedition together, when our paths occasionally cross, the Svalbard memories come flooding back.

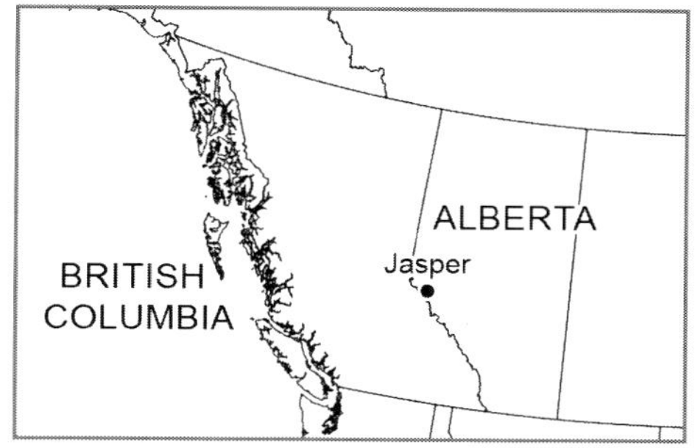

2

The Athabasca trail -
in the footsteps of David Douglas (1983)

Mix four tenderfoot explorers, a large dose of Canadian wilderness, close encounters of a wildlife kind and an ill-prepared mountain climb and you have a recipe for adventure…

"*And if a bear should approach you, just remember some good advice an old backwoodsman once told me...*" said the Canadian fisherman who had approached us, festooned with tackle, "*wait 'till he's real close - then spit in his face. That'll scare him away*". We thanked him for his comforting words of advice and watched him disappear, rod in hand, towards Moab Lake. The whole idea of being able to project sufficient spittle accurately into a bear's face as it advanced menacingly stretched even our naive credulity.

The four of us had left the car at Moab, some fifteen miles south of Jasper in the Canadian Rockies and were making last minute adjustments to backpacks in preparation for 'The Pilgrimage'. For many years the idea of following in David Douglas's footsteps had captured our imagination: at last that dream was about to be realised in an eighty-mile, six-day hike up the Athabasca Pass and back. When Douglas walked it in 1827, the route had only been in use for sixteen years. Fur trader David Thomson had pioneered this trail, which was to have great significance as the main crossing of 'The Great Divide' - the Rocky Mountain chain separating what is now British Columbia in the west from Alberta in the east. This route was used for fifty years, until the Yellowhead Pass - today's main mountain crossing - was discovered to the North West. At one time the Athabasca Pass formed part of an important commercial route for the Hudson's Bay Company Express, which regularly carried furs and other goods the two thousand miles from Fort Vancouver in Oregon to York Factory on Hudson's Bay, prior to their dispatch to the Old World. Set in some of the world's most spectacular wilderness this trail is just one of many to be explored in the Jasper National Park. The Park admits over two million visitors yearly but in 1983 this trail's maximum annual permitted quota of 300 hikers had yet to be reached. Clearly a wilderness experience then.

Why had this idea captured our imagination? Douglas was for a long time an unsung hero. Born of humble origins in Scone, near Perth in 1799, his Pacific Northwest plant-collecting expeditions under the aegis of the Royal Horticultural Society were of enormous significance to British flora in general and to British forestry in particular. Apart from his own living memorial - the Douglas fir - Douglas was responsible for introducing into Britain the Sitka spruce, Lodgepole pine, Noble and Red firs, as well as the Western white pine and Western yellow pine. Although much of 20th century USA and Canada would be unrecognisable to Douglas today, very little would have changed in the fastness of the Rocky Mountains. By retracing his footsteps and reading his diary entries we hoped to gain an inkling of the sort of personality that made up this tough, resolute and brave Scot.

Our final adjustments made, we paused to record the moment on film and then shouldered our packs for the first time. After half a mile we encountered a family who had been fishing Moab Lake. We little suspected that this group would be the last humanity we would encounter for the coming six days. Initially, the going was easy. Some years ago a fire track had been constructed to a small cabin, five miles from the start of the trail. Now with boulders placed to block vehicle access, the track was gradually deteriorating, with grass and flowers colonising what was once a sandy road. A violent rainstorm came out of nowhere, then abated as suddenly as it had started, its raindrops sparkling the surrounding vegetation with colour: clumps of purple vetch and beautiful pink wild roses, provincial emblem of Alberta.

Bordering the track were two solid, seemingly impenetrable ranks of natural Lodgepole pine. About the twisted coastal version of this pine with which he was so familiar Douglas recorded in his journals, "*Little can be said in favour of this tree either for ornament or as a useful wood*". In future it may be that Lodgepole pine will become less common in the undisturbed Canadian National Parks. Although an effective coloniser, it requires fire in order for its cones to open and hence for its released seeds to germinate. Natural fires following dry lightning strikes would normally ensure this process, but fire outbreaks occurring today - whether naturally or deliberately started - are quickly extinguished by trouble-shooting helicopter crews. Public criticism of a laissez-faire fire attitude is probably responsible for this policy. But by artificially preventing this 'natural' process it follows that no plant succession can take place, hence, no herbs and shrubs palatable to grazing animals. Over time and space the mature forest continues uninterrupted and undisturbed, and the environment effectively becomes 'sterile' for most wildlife. During our hike one noteworthy feature was this general absence of wildlife – although our deliberate noisiness may have been a contributory factor.

Our route gradually ascended roughly parallel to the Whirlpool River. Here, not far from its junction with the great Athabasca River (the so called 'Meeting of the Waters'), the turbid Whirlpool rushed northwards, too rapid and too deep to cross. Its milky-grey appearance - caused by a suspension of fine silt particles - indicated its origins as melt-water from glaciers higher up the Pass. We watched apprehensively, for we knew that some 25 miles upstream our trail would cross the unbridged river. At each turn of the fire track, fresh views appeared of the surrounding snow-covered mountains (for the greater part unnamed on the map). Apart from the rushing Whirlpool River the only sound was the continuous tinkling of our bear bells, bought previously in Jasper. This precaution relies on the theory that a bear will hear you long before he sees you and is thus given ample warning to make a sharp exit. However - as we were shortly to discover - the reality can be somewhat different from the theory...

Eventually the track made an abrupt ending and we cast around for the correct route. From now on the trail consisted of a single-file path indicated by blaze marks (tree-trunk slash marks, some evidently very old) on occasional wayside conifers. From time to time the trail would be blocked by a fallen tree ('deadfall' in the Canadian parlance) and we would have to negotiate a way over, under or around the obstacle. By now the Lodgepole pine had largely given way to white and black spruces. These close-canopied shade-bearing species afforded only the occasional glimpse of surrounding mountains, hampering our orientation. As the trail emerged at a bluff above the Whirlpool River we caught sight of an adult moose grazing on the water meadows some distance ahead, oblivious of its human spectators.

Around every hour we would break for a few minutes. Such stops were usually a mixed blessing for - especially on the lower reaches of the Athabasca Pass - hordes of ferocious mosquitoes would inexorably discover insect-repellent-free anatomy. It was at this stage of the hike that we were starting to become confident about the lack of bear evidence when, only 50 yards ahead, *Ursus americanus* (Black Bear) was seen nonchalantly ambling into the surrounding wood. Thereafter, we added periodic whistling to accompany the tinkling of our bear bells!

Nine miles up the trail lay the relics of an abandoned loggers' encampment, long disused. Roofless log cabins were slowly rotting away, whilst here and there pine and spruce seedlings were gradually reclaiming the area they had once lost to man's activities. Although this spot was almost a mile distant from the Whirlpool River we spied two flat bottomed clinker built 'York' boats of a type commonly used in Hudson's Bay during the 19th century lying half buried beside the trail. Leaving the camp's only remaining occupant - a rather disgruntled chipmunk - in peace, we continued to push our way southwards and upwards.

Having made good rate of progress that afternoon and with morale high, we once more discovered that the Rockies were not to be treated lightly. Our over-confidence was rudely shattered by the realisation that we had lost the trail beside some river flats. Retracing our steps and casting around for the route proved fruitless. A hasty consultation of the map did not help. In desperation we struck out over the deadfall, hoping to encounter the trail higher up. An hour later, plagued by mosquitoes, sweating, tired and hungry, our packs biting into shoulders and hips, and with night falling we despondently pitched camp beside the Whirlpool River and tried to sleep. A search would have to be made the next day for the elusive trail. At around 3 a.m. with the sky pitch-dark above us, we awoke with a start Outside, only yards from the tent, a stick had snapped. Sounds of something moving about were heard. Never before had tent cotton seemed so thin! The presence remained nearby for what seemed like a lifetime and then slowly moved away, leaving only the sounds of the Whirlpool River and our beating hearts. We later arose, chastened by the twin experiences of the deadfall and The Visitation. To our relief, our food supplies, carefully slung high between two trees at some distance from the camp, had remained undisturbed. After a two-hour reconnoitre, clambering through a profusion of deadfall, we eventually regained the trail again. Knowing that Douglas had suffered similar problems was little consolation (his diary for 3rd May read "*The path was extremely difficult from the dead wood and the ground still soft from the melting of the snow*").

Only after retracing the blaze marks did we realise that our camp had been pitched a mere fifty yards from the trail! Anxious to make up for lost time, we started out again. Some twenty miles up the Pass, at about 5,000 feet, the trail led along a two mile shingly flat, braided by several arms of the river. Here, the occasional stunted white spruce eked out an existence among clumps of purple vetch and mountain avens. Above the flats towered near-vertical mountain slopes, gouged out by glaciers during the last ice age, with subalpine fir clinging on to precarious footholds and finally petering out at around 1,830m (6,000 ft).

One thousand feet higher still, the remains of spring snow merged into permanent ice fields. We observed a curiously striped appearance to the mountain sides, caused by snow lingering in the folds of the slopes. Douglas noted this in his journals, "*…it is worthy of notice, however, that all I have yet seen here and west of the Rocky Mountains have a dip from 30° to 45° south west. I do not recall a single exception*". None of the surrounding peaks were named by explorers prior to 1827 and it is interesting to note that even today the official maps of the Canadian Rockies still record very few names. However, as we neared the end of the shingle, two exceptions towered in front of us: Mount Evans and Mount Kane. Paul Kane, an artist who crossed the Athabasca

Pass in 1846, produced several watercolours of the Canadian scenery. Mount Evans had been climbed shortly after Captain Scott's abortive Antarctic expedition, forming a trio along with the nearby Mt. Oates and Mt. Scott. The peak we eagerly sought - Mount Brown, a sentinel to the west of the highest point on the pass -was as yet invisible.

The morning of the third day found us roped together by the edge of the Whirlpool River, scanning for the best crossing point. Boots tied around our necks and backpack hip straps undone in case of a tumble, we each fumbled our way through the freezing water which numbed our feet and destroyed all sense of feeling. Our suffering was as nothing compared to Douglas's however. His journal for 2 May noted, "*... Crossed the river fifteen times in three places; two half full of water, very rapid and full of large stones*". Early morning is the best time to cross a glacial river. By mid-afternoon the water level can rise many inches from glacial melting by the sun. Once beyond the other side, the trail progressively deteriorated towards the upper limit of the montane zone, with deadfall increasingly hampering progress. Here and there, patches of snow reminded us that the subalpine zone was not far away. Deep swathes on the mountainsides opposite indicated where former avalanches had swept the trees away before them. Within these scars, a light green carpet of willow and mountain alder contrasted with the darker green borders of spruce. No doubt the fresh broadleaved growth made good grazing.

At 1,680m (5,500ft) carpets of alpine flowers, newly-emerged from their mantle of spring snow, covered the meadows in a profusion of yellow and white. The summit of Mount Brown now seemed very close and we knew that the head of the Pass must be even closer. Suddenly there appeared before us what we had come so far to see: three small jewels of lakes, the middle one - the 'Committee's Punchbowl' - marking the border between British Columbia and Alberta. As if on cue, a wolverine watched us from the far side, rare guardian of this secluded treasure, before silently slinking away. Even now, in late June, the Punchbowl was almost obscured by ice floes (Douglas walked the route in early May). However, this did not deter the oldest member of our group from celebrating our arrival at the top of the Athabasca Pass with a quick dip!

This historic place must have witnessed many joyful encounters during the early days of the Hudson's Bay Company. Parties of fur traders would set out from either side of the Pass, meeting at the Punchbowl to exchange mail and supplies. A curious fact noted by Douglas was that this lochan comprised a true watershed, with one outflow forming the start of the Columbia River (and thence into the Pacific) and the other forming the start of the Athabasca River (eventually reaching the Arctic). At this peaceful spot one almost sensed that time had stood still. Old blaze marks testified to generations of explorers and traders who had travelled the Pass before us, no doubt grateful to be quickening their steps once past this watershed meeting point. That evening, blue smoke from our camp fire reflected clearly in the glassy smoothness of the nearby lochan and the usually persistent mosquitoes were almost absent. The evening calm was broken only by a distant ominous rumbling of small avalanches from the slopes of Mount Brown above us. Tomorrow would see the 2,799m (9,183ft) challenge of Mount Brown itself, climbed by Douglas and noted as the first recorded ascent of a Canadian Rocky by white man.

Douglas named the peak after Robert Brown, a contemporary eminent British botanist. Douglas had greatly overestimated the height at 17,000 feet, thereby giving rise to a myth - which lasted for nearly seventy years - that Mount Brown was the highest peak in the North American continent. Not until 1843 did A. P. Coleman, Geology Professor at the University of Toronto, determine the actual height at approximately 9,000 feet. What contributed to the inaccuracy was David Thomson's incorrect estimate in 1811 of the height of the Athabasca Pass at 11,000 feet (it is in fact 1,753m (5,751ft).

The day of our ascent dawned bright and clear and we arose early to prepare for the 1,000m climb. As we made our way slowly up the snow slopes, the sun emerged from the glaciated outline of Mount Hooker to our east. Douglas named this peak after his mentor William Jones Hooker, Professor of Botany at the University of Glasgow, with whom he worked between 1820 and 1823. It was Hooker who recommended Douglas to the Horticultural Society as a plant collector and clearly he had been a great influence in shaping Douglas' career. After Douglas's death, Hooker wrote, "*...he was a diligent attendant at the botanical lectures given by the Professor of Botany in the hall of the garden and was his favourite companion in some distant excursions to the Highlands and Islands of Scotland when his great activity, undaunted courage, singular abstemiousness and energetic zeal, at once pointed him out as an individual eminently calculated to do himself credit as a scientific traveller*".

Douglas found difficulty with the first part of the ascent, "*The labour of ascending the lower part, which is covered with pines, is great beyond description, sinking on many occasions to the middle*" and what to us had appeared straightforward from the Pass turned out to be much more difficult than expected. Traces of last night's avalanches were evident and several false ridges and overhanging cornices required careful negotiations with our somewhat inadequate equipment!

As our spidery trail threaded up the pristine snow face there emerged into view legions of snow-clad peaks, the glorious Rocky Mountain range stretching far into the distance. The Punchbowl was now like a small pond far below us and our tents were mere orange and brown specks. We paused for a birds-eye perspective of the forest through which we had threaded for three days. Kicking steps in the snow we eventually gained the top of the ridge. And what a panorama greeted us! On all horizons nothing but mountains, glaciers and snow: not a trace of man or man's activities. One could understand Douglas's elation, recorded in his journal for 1st May 1827, "*Nothing, as far as the eye could perceive, but mountains such as 1 was on, and many higher, some rugged beyond any description, striking the mind with horror blended with a sense of the wondrous works of the Almighty. The aerial tints of the snow, the heavenly azure of the solid glaciers, the rainbow-like lines of their thin broken fragments, the huge mossy icicles hanging from the perpendicular rocks with the snow sliding from the steep southern rocks with amazing velocity, producing a crash and grumbling like the shock of an earthquake, the echo of which resounding in the valley for several minutes*".

Although our prize - the summit itself - was now only 150m (500ft) higher, it lay almost a mile to our northwest. The ridge ascent had taken longer than expected, we were unsure of the exact route down and the sky was clouding over ominously. Reluctantly, we made the decision to turn our backs on Mount Brown and begin our descent...

Douglas experienced many hardships during his hike through the Athabasca Pass. The day following his Mount Brown climb he wrote, "*My ankles and knees pained me so much from exertion that my sleep was short and interrupted*". Towards the end of his short life he was much troubled by poor eyesight, of which a contributing factor may have been partial snow-blindness following the ascent of Mount Brown. Possibly failing eyesight may also have contributed to his premature and tragic death. He was only thirty five years old when - in Hawaii - he fell into a pit dug for wild cattle and was gored to death.

With all the benefits of modern technology, our hardships on the trail were undoubtedly fewer. By undertaking this pilgrimage in the footsteps of David Douglas we had hoped to gain some small understanding of this remarkable man. But after arriving back at Jasper and civilisation some days later we realised that this had been only part of our wilderness experience. We had also come to understand a little more about ourselves.

The other members of this expedition consisted of my wife Rachel, Richard Colbeck, undergraduate at the University of Edinburgh, and the late John Davies, O.B.E., formerly Forestry Commission Conservator South Scotland.

Athabasca Trail

The Athabasca Trail

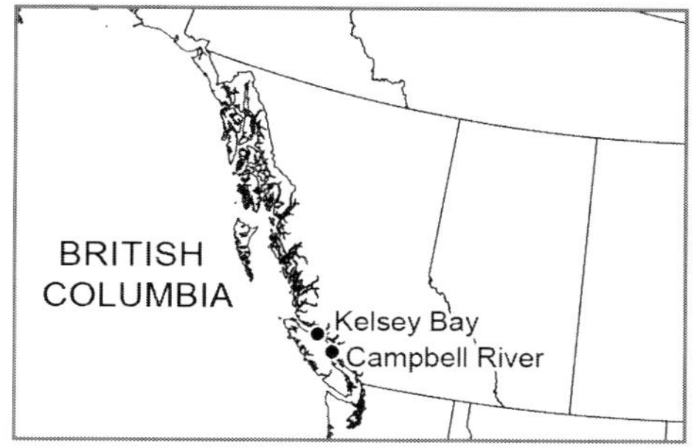

3

Family Adventures in Canada (1994)

Think that fishing is a quiet, unadventurous pursuit? Think again…

We visited British Columbia in search of adventure, but what we found was Elsie.

Don't get me wrong. Adventures were there: adventures a-plenty. But Elsie was in a league of her own. She surpassed everything with ease…

It all started in what the Canadians call the 'village' of Campbell River, a community of around 27,000 souls situated halfway up the east side of Vancouver Island, in BC. Was it possible, we wondered, to experience a family holiday which combined adventures and excitement on the one hand, with routine and relaxation on the other? How could the needs of a five- and six-year-old girl and boy be reconciled with the more adventurous expectations of their parents?

In the event we needn't have worried. British Columbia is the adventure holidaymaker's Shangri-La, a vast Province four times the size of Britain itself, where the pioneering spirit is still alive and kicking and where the great outdoors is a way of life for most, not just wishful thinking. Whatever your age, whatever your fitness, you can do almost anything here given the inclination, the time and a few dollars. Hiking, mountain biking, whale-watching, white water rafting, sailing, riding - it's all there for the taking, in what every auto licence plate continually reminds you (as if you needed reminding) is *Beautiful British Columbia*.

One of Campbell River's claims to fame is its international reputation as 'salmon capital of the world'; the other is a newspaper called (surprise, surprise) - Salmon News. Volume 14 number 3 carries an article about Tyee, giant salmon over 30lbs in weight, highly prized by the visiting fishing clientele. We were due to meet expert local guide Harley Elias, an irrepressible optimist. "*We'll take the family out for an afternoon's fishing trip and then you and I will go catch a tyee,*" he said to me nonchalantly, with a supreme and - as it happened - totally misplaced confidence in our angling abilities. The time had come to disabuse Harley. Quickly, I briefed him on our family's collective skills, knowledge and experience in the realm of fishing, accurately summed up by the term 'non-existent'. This - Harley assured me - was not a problem.

One hour and one permit later, we found ourselves out on the sunny coastal waters of Discovery Passage in a small fibreglass boat. On one side there rose the hauntingly beautiful coastline foreground of Van' Island, leading up to ridge after serrated ridge of rugged forested slopes. On the other side there rose vertically from the sea a cliff- or 'bluff' as the Canadians call it, topped - cliché fashion - with a lonesome pine. To complete the picture, a bald eagle (not really bald, but like all bald eagles sporting a white punk feather head-dress) perched on a branch of this pine tree and looked disdainfully down on us. While we cast our herring-baited lines over the side of the boat, it cast its disapproving gimlet gaze on our amateur fishing efforts.

But almost immediately the eagle was forgotten, as a taut line indicated a bite. Angling fever suddenly swept the boat as we became gripped in the drama of a mighty combat between small boy and big fish. Or so we thought...

Unfortunately the marine monster turned out to be not a sockeye, coho, pink, chum or mighty chinook - all salmon for which this area is famous - but a diminutive ling cod instead. Undeterred however, we celebrated our first successful capture by throwing the hapless cod towards the bald eagle in a small gesture of international friendship, a symbolic peace offering between man and bird (or so we thought). We wanted to make restitution for having strayed into the eagle's terrestrial waters. Contrarily, the king of the birds merely continued to preen itself with conspicuous hauteur, so we readdressed the serious subject of salmon fishing. Several dogfish later ("*Look what we've caught- another shark!*" shouted the triumphant kids) a reluctant cod was hauled aboard, flapping around in the bottom of the boat until Harley swiftly dispatched it with a cedar wood truncheon rejoicing in the name of a 'fish bonker'. We threw the cod towards the bald eagle and waited once again for a dramatic action-packed water swoop. This time the regal raptor glided listlessly downwards in a half-hearted display of interest, but decided at the last moment not to take its bonked victim. Perhaps it was beneath its dignity.

To be honest, having visited BC to research a book on adventure holidays, I had found this fishy business to be a wee bit on the tame side so far, but nothing prepared me for the terrifying evening sequel to the afternoon's angling expedition: Harley's (literally) lightning tour of northern Discovery Passage. After dropping the rest of the family back on shore, he and I set off to negotiate the dangers of this turbulent stretch of water and continue the search for our elusive salmon. To the inexperienced, the fierce tidal swirls, eddies, rapids, rocks and whirlpools which characterise this convoluted strait, are potentially vicious killers. Many lives have been lost here in the past and you still have to treat these waters with a strong health warning even with today's sophisticated navigational aids. In daylight, in a small open boat such as ours, without such aids, you have to know what you're doing. Night trips are definitely not recommended. Thus it was that a few hours - and several more dogfish - later, just as we were giving up hope of hooking that ever-elusive salmon, the sky suddenly blackened over without warning as a vicious thunderstorm appeared from nowhere.

Torrential rain began to lash down, steadily filling the small craft. Thunderbolts crashed down everywhere, some much too close for comfort. A number hit the nearby forest, lighting up the spruce trees like some dramatic Wagnerian stage effect. These lightning strikes were so close we could even smell the odour of zapped sap.

Our eventual return in the pitch dark, through an evil tidal rip, via an unscheduled stop at an uninhabited island, is another tale in itself, the human equivalent of 'the ones that got away'. Suffice to say that Harley - who had lived in the area most of his life - had never experienced the like of this storm before. He was as relieved as I when we eventually reached the safety of Painters Lodge that night. "*Well, you never did get to catch your salmon*" he remarked, when it was all over, "*but at least we had an adventure!*" I made a mental note to avoid any more fishing in the future – my normally adventurous disposition simply couldn't take it, never mind what my insurers would think.

By now the phantom Campbell River salmon seemed more like virtual reality than flesh and blood fish so when the chance came to see them in their natural environment, I jumped at it. Campbell River Snorkel Tours is operated by Steve Farrer, a laconic, laid-back diver and jack of all trades who for a few dollars will kit you out in wetsuit, fins, mask and snorkel, and let you 'play fish' for a day. It's a unique underwater adventure to drift downstream with the steady five mph current ("*Like being on a mobile water-bed*" Steve explained) whilst thousands of migrating salmon push past you in the opposite direction - a sort of fishy commuter rush. Seeing a 70lb 4ft long salmon close enough to touch is remarkable: the spectacle of thousands of migrating salmon brushing past you in the river is, well, spectacular. A few hundred people experience this tour each year and many make a return trip. "*I've taken everyone from a six year old kid to a seventry two year old grandmother*" explained Steve. "*Everyone's nervous on the way out- the van's quiet and tense. But afterwards you can't stop 'em talking about it, they're so excited.*" I asked about the 72-year-old grandmother. "*Elsie, her name is*" he said. "*She only learnt to swim in her sixties and she walks on crutches. Had a wetsuit made especially for her after her first snorkel run here. She's been back several times since.*"

I was beginning to like the sound of Elsie.

No holiday on Vancouver Island would be complete without a whale-watching excursion. Strictly speaking, orcas - or killer whales - aren't whales at all and neither do they kill human beings. *Orchinus orca* is a member of the dolphin family and 330 of them live off the Pacific Northwest coast, mainly in families or 'pods'. John Ganzner is the tanned, likeable, no-frills operator of Robson Bight Charters based at Kelsey Bay on northeast Vancouver Island. Most days during the summer his 56ft motor boat *Le Caique* takes up to thirty passengers of all ages through some of the most spectacularly beautiful scenery you will find on this planet. For a few dollars, his seafaring safari will take you in search of seals, eagles, bears, dolphins and of course, killer whales.

When the family joined this whale-watching expedition we started with high hopes, but the hours drifted past and never an orca was there to be seen. Four hours after leaving Kelsey Bay we'd all given up the thought of glimpsing one. But not so John. He was determined not to disappoint us and as luck would have it, just as we were about to head back, his sixth-sea-sense located them in the distance. When we drew alongside, the whales themselves seemed almost as excited as we were. The ship's hydrophones positively chattered with an assortment of clicks, hisses and whistles ('vocalizations' as the Canadians prosaically call this advanced communication system). Each pod is distinctive and - to the experts at least - easily recognised. Pod T36 which we had come so far to see, consisted of four orcas in a closely-knit family group.

Watching whales is a mesmeric experience. After what seemed like only five minutes, John insisted that we finish taking photographs. The five minutes had in fact been at least an hour and we had a long way to get back home. And so at last, with reluctance we turned tail ourselves and headed for home. Chugging back through the strait we dodged the showers, the commercial fishing boats and an occasional Canadian log barge ('west coast hay waggons', as the loggers call them). In the distance more rain could be seen sweeping towards us. It was then that I spotted an old lady I hadn't noticed before. She sat alongside skipper John, on the exposed wheel-deck admiring the view. I could see she was enjoying the trip, for despite her soaking she seemed enthralled at the spectacle, alert to everything around her. Ignoring the rain myself, I approached her and started to make conversation. She was a remarkable lady, so content, and yet so full of life and spirit and adventure for one evidently getting on in years. I asked her what her name was and she told me what I already knew instinctively.

"*Elsie*", she said with a twinkle in her eye.

I had somehow felt sure that our paths would cross and sure enough, here she was: none other than Elsie - the snorkeller, the grandmother, the adventurer. As the sun finally emerged from behind the clouds, a rainbow swept its triumphant, life-affirming arch overhead, perfectly framing her frail but vital figure. The boat was approaching Kelsey Bay once more and we were approaching the end of our family adventure on Vancouver Island. "*Have you lived in Canada all your life?*" I asked her, before we parted company.

Her piercing blue eyes smiled up at me and she replied with a chuckle, "*Not yet*".

With Imogen, Charles and Rachel on an unforgettable family expedition (and no, none of us have since taken up angling…)

British Columbia
HYAK

4

Happily River Rafter (1994)

Rafting may be a 'wet world at my feet', but it can be every bit as exciting as climbing...

Our twelve person crew consisted mainly of young female students from the Far East and Mexico. English was most definitely their second language. We also had a non-swimmer and a couple of self-confessed wimps. Practically none of us had been in a raft before. Now, as our 18ft inflatable dinghy cast off slowly and inexorably down the mighty Thompson River in British Columbia's 'High Country' interior, we all tried not to dwell on our shortcomings - or on the rapids awaiting us downstream. '*The Frog*' didn't sound too bad but what about the '*Witches Cauldron*' or the '*Devil's Kitchen*' or the spine-chilling '*Jaws of Death*'? Hardly reassuring names, especially after we'd all signed an indemnity form in the event of personal injury - or worse. But we didn't have much time to dwell on the macabre, for Joanne - our strong, blonde and capable river guide - was completing her briefing...

"*If you fall overboard, your first priority is to stay with the raft.*" she explained. "*Cling onto the side ropes or hook the T bar of your paddle onto someone else's on board. If that doesn't work I'll throw you a life-line. Like this.*" She demonstrated with all the insouciance of an air hostess running through a standard emergency drill. But we were not reassured and by now the first rapids were approaching like an express train. Listening intently, we sat astride the raft's inflatable sides, one leg dangling impotently in the river, the other fixed in a foot loop, our paddles poised, ready for white-water action. Then, upon command, we paddled furiously but ineffectually towards '*The Frog*', holding our breath and waiting for the inevitable deluge...

Two centuries ago, when Alexander MacKenzie encountered the turbulent, glacier-fed rivers flowing from Canada's Rocky Mountains, they must have struck him as a mightily forbidding spectacle, but like the original native peoples who passed here before him and the white settlers who followed afterwards, MacKenzie realised that it was the river and lake systems of this vast country which literally held the solution to Canada's communication problems. These natural arteries could provide a vital means by which to link the Pacific Northwest with the Atlantic seaboard. Although railways - and later highways - eventually displaced waterways as means of transportation, use of British Columbia's rivers by ships, rafts and canoes flourished for decades. Nowadays it's adventure tourism which fuels this use, and, like never before, white water rafting is in demand.

One's first taste of rafting is unforgettable. There's an utter and glorious confusion of surging spray, roaring waves and frantic instructions, combined with the savage force of an angry and foaming maelstrom. The experience is sometimes terrifying, often awesome, always exhilarating. For many it's this adrenalin rush which brings them back regularly for their white water fix. But it's wrong to imagine that rafting is the sole preserve of twenty-something mucho macho honchos: our mainly female crew was visible evidence of that. Indeed, one of the trip's many surprises was seeing children of all ages - from ten to seventy - out on the river, tripping out on their Thompson 'high'. It's not just the buffeting bangs which you get for your bucks either. Many operators provide a gourmet lunch on some calm riverside beach, partway through the trip. It's only then that you can really relax and start to appreciate the eerie hoodoo scenery of BC's dry interior sierra: gaunt pinnacles of rock perched on steeply incised canyons whose upper slopes are clad with sparse pine trees and sagebrush bushes. Here the peacefulness is cathartic, although every now and then the stillness is shattered by the bizarre booming of loco horn-blasts and the high pitched squealing of box-car axles as sinuous railroad freight trains snake their way high up above you on precipitous rock ledges.

Early traders feared and respected the Thompson rapids, making long and laborious 'portages' in order to avoid them. Today, these same rapids are still feared and respected, but they're also challenged, embraced and conquered by white-water aficionados. Whole ranges of craft ply these waters during the season (May to September). We saw short stubby kayaks sliding along on the crests of the waves, their skilful paddlers occasionally flipping into an eskimo roll on quiet river stretches, cooling off like so many dabbling ducks. At the other end of the spectrum were the giant inflatable rigs, powered by outboard motors, holding as many as twenty people.

Other rafts were smaller, paddle-only affairs, their guide steering from the stem. Our inflatable was steered by oars, with Joanne sitting on a centre seat helping to row the raft as well as steering it.

As each successive rapid became larger and larger, Joanne (by now rechristened the River Goddess) berated us for not putting enough effort into it. "*If I shout at you it's not because I'm angry with you*," she explained "*it's because we all need to paddle like hell in order to shoot the rapids*". The theory goes that you have to be travelling faster than the rapids themselves in order to get through; if not you run the risk of stopping mid-stream (a sort of waterfall water-stall) after which there's a very real danger of the raft being flipped over by a wave. Twenty years ago, when there were sixty or so operators in British Columbia, many untrained, some inexperienced and a few downright unsafe, it was a rafting disaster waiting to happen, and happen it did. Two inflatables capsized in the mid-1980s, with considerable loss of life. But although tragic at the time, those deaths did lead to legislation which resulted in tight government control over the rafting industry. Now BC's thirty five or so companies require a licence to operate and are subject to stringent, unannounced inspections by government officials. Equipment, training and safety procedures are checked and fines or licence withdrawals imposed on culprits. The result is that Canada's rafting industry is probably the safest and most professional in the world today.

Meanwhile, back on the river, we were attacking the '*Witches Cauldron*' with gusto, whooping with exhilaration, soaked to the skin. As rapid succeeded rapid, our fear of the great white walls of water gradually diminished, thanks to the encouragement of the River Goddess and the support of each other. Even when crew member Cathy spilled overboard in the middle of a rapid, our rescue response and teamwork were exemplary. For here was another unexpected marvel: what had started out as a disparate collection of non-swimmers, wimps and aquaphobes ended up forty kilometers later as a unified and united team. Sure, we were only Lilliputians fighting against the mighty Thompson, but we had been literally thrown together by the experience, team-bonded by the powerful river's still mightier power. And in the end courage triumphed over fear.

"*Who wants to jump out and hold on to the rope down the next rapid*?" asked Joanne. "I*t's your last chance before we finish*". Five hours ago we'd have been superglued to our seats. Now we all leapt into the water faster than spray off a paddle - even our non-swimming crew member...

But all good things come to an end and all too soon, Lytton - rafting capital of Canada - hove into sight around a comer. Our white water adventure was over, but only for the time being. We'd be back for more - happily. River-rafting's like that.

Cathy Hasell – whom we met in Lesotho – is Godmother to son Charles and a veritable aquaphile.

Kilimanjaro

5
The Snows of Kilimanjaro (1997)

This rather audacious trip to 'Kili' lit a spark that inadvertently kindled my seven summits quest…

Looking back some twenty years, little did I suspect in 1997 when faced with a spare week's leave, that a spontaneous African adventure would trigger a life-changing quest to climb all the continents' highest summits. But, in truth, that's how it all started.

Randomly surfing the net one day revealed a cheap Sabena return flight to Kenya. Seats available - tick.

A quick phone call to Bridget King who lived in Nairobi. Yes I could stay - tick.

Assemble kit - tick.

And suddenly it was a case of '*game on; Kilimanjaro here I come.*'

After an enjoyable day spent looking for obsidian with Bridget in Hell's Gate Park she casually remarked, "*If you're going to climb Kili you'd better get a move on: it usually takes several days and you've only got a week left.*" Thus began a ridiculously serendipitous few days of my life where everything seemed to click into place with effortless ease, each lucky step conspiring with the next towards ultimate success…

Occasionally Africa can be like that.

This series of fortunate events started with a bizarre but fruitful journey from Kenya's capital by car, bus and matatus (privately owned minibuses) across the Tanzanian border to Arusha. All the while the distinctive volcanic cone of Africa's highest mountain rose up like – well, frankly, like an empress above the Serengeti. Finally I reached the village of Moshi on Kili's lower slopes where I walked the last half mile up to the reception of the Jacaranda B&B.

"*Have you a reservation Sir?*"

I hadn't.

A barely disguised look of amusement flitted over the receptionist's face. This wasn't looking very good for me. But, wait a minute, there had been a recent cancellation and a room was in fact available – result! I then explained that I wanted to climb The Mountain. So far so good. But when I explained that this would mean my having to set out the next morning there was much amusement from the receptionist, this time undisguised.

"*Everyone books many days in advance Sir*," she laughed, "*Sometimes months.*"

Things were starting to unravel. In desperation, feeling like the Elephant's Child in Kipling's Just-So Stories, I kept asking questions, half expecting to get a beating for my 'satiable curtiosity'.

"*Who can help me*?"

"*Where can I get hold of a guide?*"

"*Is anyone going from here?*"

"*Well you could talk to that group over there.*" The receptionist gestured outside. "*They might be able to help…?*"

Thanking her, I wandered over to a corner of the B&B grounds where a rather travel-worn overland group had pitched their tents. It turned out that they had set out in a truck from London several weeks before and were en route to Nairobi. But in the meantime they were here, intending to climb Kilimanjaro and, as it happened, planning to start tomorrow morning. A few beers later and they graciously accepted my request to join them. Oh frabjous day! Things were looking up again. Literally.

There are several trails up the mountain but the overlanders had opted for the popular Marangu route. Again, serendipity for me, since this 'tourist trail' could be done in in five days: one day less than the other routes. Any longer for me and I'd have missed my flight home. But, as the guide books pointed out, '*The Marangu route is not always the best way, due to a shorter acclimatisation period*'.

Left to their own devices, or with unscrupulous guides, inexperienced climbers ascend Kilimanjaro far too quickly, getting past the half-way mark and then 'hitting the wall': that's to say suffering from the effects of altitude and having to turn back. As a newbie to 'getting high' I surely would have done so. And so the next stroke of luck in this series of fortunate events was that the overland group leader, a twice-failed-determined-to-make-it-third-time-lucky white Rhodesian who resolutely refused to accept Zimbabwe as a reality and took an extreme view of what it means to climb gradually. Our group mantra became the Swahili phrase 'pole, pole' (slowly, slowly) and so we shuffled upwards like a collective of sloths (although a sloth is - confusingly - a collective of bears. But I digress…).

Although the passage of time has dulled my memory of the ascent's nuances, some things still remain clearly etched in my mind: the climb up from Marangu Gate to Mandara huts through misty montane forests, their Ent-like branches festooned with bearded mosses dripping with moisture; up past giant lobelias and groundsel towards Horombo huts and the moorlands; then on through Alpine desert to the stone built Kibo hut. Some things stand out particularly, like the voice of an angel: one of our party who would nightly serenade us to sleep with beautiful jazz songs much better than could have any mere Walkman. But by the time we reached Kibo, we were all - to a greater or lesser extent - nauseous and headachy, unable to sleep and full of trepidation for what the next 1,200m (4,000ft) might bring…

Setting out in darkness we could see the glow-worm lights from other groups already above us, zig-zagging their way up the ash clinker path. This part of the climb seemed to go on for ever. As the guide book puts it '*This section is very steep with a lot of stone scree, requiring great physical and mental effort. This is probably the most demanding section of the entire route.*' But the appearance of the almost full moon gave us a perspective on our upward progress and provided a welcome psychological boost. After what felt like an eternity of upward footsteps, all of a sudden one's vertical world levelled off. We had reached Gilman's Point, on the crater rim! Sure we were all feeling oxygen-challenged and generally spaced-out, but from here on it was only a gradual 200m ascent past spectacular ice formations to Uhuru peak at 5,895m (19,341ft). And when we did finally get there, the views from the world's highest free-standing mountain were incomparable. On all sides stretched the distant haze of the African plains and - over forty miles away and well below us - wisps of cloud cloaked the top of Mount Meru (4,565m/14,977ft). But the roof of Africa is no place to linger when the breeze is picking up and we had a lot of descending to do…

The best scree slope in the world has to be Kilimanjaro's volcanic cone, but, frustratingly I could only take a few giant leaps downward before having to stop, lungs heaving with exertion, desperate for oxygen. But the lower you get, the richer the air becomes, so that by the time Kibo hut reappeared, normal service was restored. By now a nagging doubt was creeping into my bubble of euphoria – how was I going to get back to Nairobi in time for my return flight?

It might seem unbelievable but in truth this is what happened. On my way down, a chance conversation with another climber revealed the fact that he was on his honeymoon – without his wife as it happened, since she got cold feet (about getting married, that is). Rather than call off the upmarket, paid-for holiday (safari, Kili, beaches: the whole nine yards) he thought he'd do it solo. So, yes, there was a Landover waiting at the bottom of the mountain and, yes, he was being driven to Nairobi and, yes, I was welcome to come along. Result! I promptly bade farewell to my climbing buddies who had proved to be such good company for the last few days, and jumped ship. But this wasn't the last of Africa's series of fortunate events…

Maybe the reason Sabena ended up going bankrupt was because of their lousy booking system. As I boarded the London-bound aircraft that evening I found my seat already occupied by another similarly-dishevelled traveller. Sabena had managed to issue two tickets for the same seat. The air hostess was duly summoned to sort things out. She took one look at the occupant and another at me and eventually beckoned me forward. My mind raced. "*Would I be summarily ejected from the plane and made to board the next one?*" But all fears were allayed when she showed me – not to the boarding steps, but to a seat in first class. Score! Now I was one happy – if rather tired – camper. So tired in fact that my only memories of the flight were answering "*Yes*" to the question "*Would Sir like some champagne and caviar?*" and then waking up as we landed at Heathrow. No first class freebies there then, but a great night's sleep and a feeling of wellbeing. Kili conquered. As Ernest Hemingway put it in *The Snows of Kilimanjaro and Other Stories*, "*that was the end of the beginning of that*".

But my mind was already wondering to itself, "*I wonder what happens after 'the end of the beginning of that'?*"

I remain in contact with Elly Douglas-Hamilton. Elly - one of the overland expedition that graciously accepted me into their climbing group – initially through her work on squirrel conservation with the Scottish Wildlife Trust and more recently through her Archerfield Walled Garden bistro and farm shop enterprise.

Kilimanjaro

6

An Aconcagua Adventure (2000)

The highest mountain outside Asia almost proved to be a climb too far when weather and fatigue took their toll…

"*What's it like to be the highest person on earth?*" shouted 'Uli' – our guide.

"*Um.*" I replied faintly.

Despite a howling gale, the thought of sleep was irresistible. I started to lie down on the summit rocks. Just a wee snooze, just forty winks, just a good doze that's all, I thought to myself, when - "*OK*" Uli shouted abruptly, "*Get up. Now. No time for sleep.*" His hand swept over a landscape of serrated snow-crowned peaks lying far below. "*We go down now.*"

I groaned, tried to concentrate on not sleeping, and eventually dragged my protesting body to an upright position. Climbing Aconcagua had been the hardest physical thing I'd ever done: the descent wasn't going to be a barrel of laughs either.

It wasn't until base camp that I remembered what Ulysses, our expert Argentinian guide, had said at the top of the 6,961m (22,837ft) peak - the highest point in the western and southern hemispheres, and therefore one of the seven summits. The theory is that since January is summer in Argentina but winter in the Himalayas, nobody would be summiting the high Himalayan peaks at that time. Aconcagua is the highest place outside the Himalayas; ergo if you're on the top, you're the highest person on earth.

Well, that's the theory anyway.

The adventure all started back in 1997 when I nicked off for a week to climb Kilimanjaro - Africa's highest point. Another day, another story, but it did make me think "*If Kili, why not Aconcagua, the world's highest trekking peak? After all it's only another Munro (ie 3,000ft) higher.*" (That was my optimistic side speaking. Perhaps my realistic side should have said, "*Yes, well maybe that's true but it's also 'only' two Munros short of Everest, and that makes it a pretty serious summit*".)

But the idea had taken hold and wouldn't go away and so I started to make plans. I was attracted to Jagged Globe the British operator — specialising in serious summits. Offering an impressive portfolio (including the seven summits) and a reputation for professionalism, this company was the obvious choice.

The goal and the means sorted, it was then a question of timing. A Jagged Globe Aconcagua trip was scheduled for 2nd January 2000. Five other people had booked. They needed six to make it viable. It was a good time to go. "*Fate must be at work here,*" I said to myself as I signed on the dotted line.

Want to know the perfect way to start a new millennium? OK, you're stretched out in a jumbo jet, sipping a G&T, watching the sunny pampas glide by below and thinking about all that wonderful wine you'll drink when you arrive in Mendoza.

Want to know what threatens the perfect start? Thoughts of millennium bugs attacking on-board computer systems, followed by thoughts of tackling a mountain not much lower than the seat in which you're reclining.

From the roadhead close to the Chilean Border, to base camp at 4,300m (14,000ft), it's a gentle - though atmospherically challenged - trek. The mules do all the donkey work (*sorry*), portering your kit thirteen miles along immense, barren and stony landscapes, but from base camp you have to shanks pony (OK I'll stop now) all your stuff yourself: tents, sleeping bags, food - the lot. Jagged Globe made a virtue out of this necessity by calling it an acclimatisation programme. I called it blinking hard work. 'Climb high and sleep low' is the ideal approach to acclimatisation, but it doesn't half entail a lot of retracing footsteps, I can tell you. Jagged Globe? Shaggèd Bloke, more like.

There's no vegetation beyond about 3,400m (11,000ft) in the Cordillera. Maurice Herzog called the lower reaches of Aconcagua '*a chaos of unstable rocks, a succession of dry slopes*' whilst the leader of an early (1897) expedition - one Edward Fitzgerald - referred to it as '*an intolerably monotonous rubbish heap*' (maybe he was just having a bad day). But to me the lack of greenery - combined with vertical rock formations, harsh sunlight and cloudless skies - created an extraordinary beautiful canvas of animated shapes, patterns and forms, changing imperceptibly with the sun's diurnal movement. It was like standing at the bottom of the Grand Canyon and looking up (except that there was a lot of snow above you).

Undoubtedly the big drawback in this part of the world is the wind. 'El viento blanco', they call it - the white wind - and it shrieks in off the Pacific (only ninety miles away) like a giant screaming skytrain, scraping snow off the slopes, shredding tents to pieces and chilling all living things in its path. The temperature on the summit is -10°C on a good day. A bad day would be -25°C. Add a pinch of jetstream and the windchill is unimaginable. It's this wind, plus the altitude, that snatches away the hopes of most would-be summiteers. Of the three thousand or so climbers who attempt Aconcagua every year, less than a third make it to the top. Several succumb to frostbite and, worse still, a dozen or so lose their lives through accident and altitude sickness. Our group was lucky: two of us summited in the end, while four turned back at various stages, suffering from the effects of altitude but during the time that we were there seven other people had paid the mountain's ultimate price.

Near the roadhead, on the way back to Mendoza, we stopped at the cemetery dedicated to Aconcagua's victims, and gave thanks for our safe delivery. Here, the poignant collection of graves, plaques and crosses was a salutary reminder of man's insignificance in the face of nature.

But Mother Nature had been merciful to me on Aconcagua, and after one failed attempt which was thwarted by the wind, I eventually reached the summit on January 19th. Although Tree Aid benefited financially, my personal enrichment from climbing Aconcagua was immeasurable. As a climbing magazine recently described the Aconcagua experience: *"When the Sentry of Stone sparkles in front of us over an ocean of summits, glaciers and gorges, a shiver will run through us in the knowledge that we leave a piece of our life here..."*

Such adventures are beyond price.

Even after she decided to abandon summit plans, Erica Newman - one of the expedition members – continued to be supportive, and we remain in occasional contact.

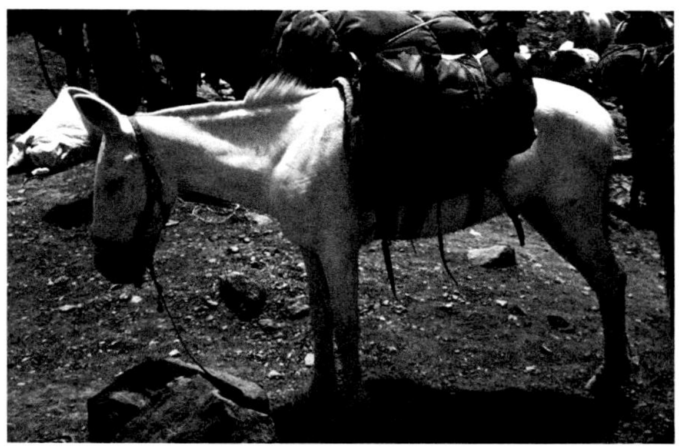

Aconcagua

Aconcagua

7

Rwenzori Rendezvous (2003)

Self-organised expeditions with friends are always the best ones. Our mainly expat forestry team spent several happy days climbing the misty mountains of 'Africa's Switzerland'...

Halfway through the expedition I proffered my Walkman to Nelson, our expedition cook. With great excitement he took the earphones, placed them reverently in his ears and concentrated on the orchestral symphony playing inside his head. His eyes lit up as he grinned at me and said in a very loud voice "*Old music!*"

Mozart would have turned in his grave.

Taking a Walkman to the Rwenzoris was a good idea, mind you. With six different huts and seven fellow adventurers, our combined nocturnal snores, sniffs and snuffles – not to mention inevitable trips outside to the loo – needed some serious muffling at times. Mozart wasn't such an odd choice of composer actually. When combined with bizarre scenery, weird flora and the effects of altitude, his 'old music' seemed somehow to complement the whole surreal experience perfectly.

The Rwenzoris form Africa's highest range of mountains. True, Mts. Kilimanjaro and Kenya are higher, but they're really geological remnants of once massive volcanoes that spewed forth from the Central Plains aeons ago. At one time the Rwenzoris formed just another flat African savannah, supporting zebras and gazelles and lions; but huge tectonic pressure, exerted over centuries, pushed up the plains from horizontal to near vertical – giving rise to their description as 'The Switzerland of Africa'. What remains today is a steep, rugged and deeply incised landscape, gouged out by the erosive effects of glaciers and rivers. Although Africa's Switzerland lies only twenty miles from the equator, its glaciers remain to this day, though much shrunken by the effects of global warming. When God combined the Rwenzoris' fantastic flora, hidden remoteness and rugged scenery, he created a 'lost world' film set that would have delighted both Richard and David Attenborough (though for different reasons).

It was the Greeks – or more accurately Ptolemy – who first postulated the existence of Africa's *lunae montes* or 'Mountains of the Moon'. "*This would be the source of the mighty Nile*" said Ptolemy, and although only conjecturing, he was proved right in 1876 when one Henry Stanley first recorded seeing these mountains. Then - as now - their glorious snow-caps remained elusive, tantalisingly veiled by drifts of cloud or mist, affording only the briefest glimpse of jagged peaks, snow-glistening summits and hostile terrain. The rainfall in this corner of Africa is a staggering three metres each year: hardly surprising, then, that the name Rwenzori stands for 'rain-maker'. It's this wetness and remoteness which have proved the Rwenzoris' saving grace, for other, more accessible African mountains have become loved to death by the footprints of countless western adventure seekers. Unlike Kilimanjaro, which attracts thousands of visitors each year, the Rwenzoris draw fewer than 150. Although this low number is due mainly to the difficulties of getting there, particular problems with Congo insurgents (that's guerillas, not gorillas) closed the National Park until two years ago. Happily, these political troubles are now over within the Park itself, although all expeditions are accompanied by an armed guard (just in case)…

It was KK - an expatriate rural development advisor working in Uganda - who first suggested the idea of a Rwenzori rendezvous. With characteristic efficiency and energy, she tirelessly organised - and reorganised - logistics, provisions and kit-lists for the eight members of the expedition. Five of the group were already based in Kampala – Uganda's capital – and most of us had forestry connections of one kind or another. It was inevitable that 'trail talk' tended towards 'tree talk', so much so in fact, that after a few days, the non-foresters tried to ban the subject of forestry outright (funnily enough they were unsuccessful).

Expeditions setting out on the Ugandan side of the Rwenzoris assemble in a small village called Nyakalangija. Pre-departure preparations are obviously regarded as a spectator sport here. Half the village turned out, to be entertained and amused by the antics of the mad mzungus (Europeans). Expedition tempers frayed as porters tried to weigh packs twice and officials attempted to inflate Park fees and Peak fees, but once the kerfuffle had finally died down and the porters had shouldered their packs, the eight of us posed for 'one last photo', then set off upwards and onwards into the unknown.

Although the going is alternately very steep and very boggy, at least climbers can enjoy the relative comfort of staying in huts – a legacy of the Mountain Club of Uganda. OK, some of them are a bit ropey and most of them have a resident population of small, hungry rodents; but not having to put up tents every night was a definite bonus. Or so we thought. During our first night in a hut – Nyabitaba – we were all woken at regular intervals by the sound of gunshot. Well actually it was louder than that. But what we all thought was a rifle in fact turned out to be the fruits of *Podocarpus milanjianus* (which are the size of small acorns) landing on the corrugated iron roof at irregular, nerve-jangling intervals. After the umpteenth cannonade, most of us were thinking "*Perhaps canvas would have been better after all*". Still, at least we had the huts mostly to ourselves... if you ignored the rats, that is (oh, and the ghostly wails of nearby hyraxes…)

The names of these huts reflected previous Rwenzori enthusiasts - like Guy Yeoman and John Matte; or local names - like Bigo and Kitandara. Some of these structures dated back to the 1940s, the materials painstakingly carried on the backs of porters and constructed in situ by the Mountain Club of Uganda. On a 1:50,000 scale map the huts appear reassuringly close, but on the ground the distance separating them is considerable. Given all the ups and downs of the terrain, it usually took around seven hours of hiking each day to get from one hut to the next. Although we were able to enjoy the comparative civilisation of these structures, the pioneer explorers had no such comforts, having to contend with canvas, caves or rock shelters. At one point along the trail we were greatly excited to discover daubed on the wall of a natural rock overhang the legend 'D d A 1906'. Although a number of climbers visited the area after Stanley's late 19th century reports, the man who literally put the Rwenzoris on the map was the Italian explorer Prince Luigi Amadeo di Savoia, the Duke of Abruzzi. In 1906 he mounted a large expedition comprising biologists, surveyors, a geologist and a photographer. They managed to summit most of the peaks and the net result was an excellent map of the Rwenzoris which was used for many years afterwards. The Duke's photographs have also been of immense scientific value, showing for example how much greater in extent were the glaciers 100 years ago than today.

If you want to climb in the Rwenzori National Park, it's best to dodge the two rainy seasons (mid-March to May, and September to mid-December) otherwise the mists can be ubiquitous, the visibility poor and the bogs? well ...*boggy*. In choosing February 2003 we were lucky: only an occasional brief downpour showed us what misery might have been. Although the local porters and guides were dressed for the wet, with welly boots of varying quality, they coped with the trail's demands amazingly well, rock-hopping over moraines and tussock-hopping over bogs with sure-footed agility. Happily for us there was no shortage of porters willing to take the strain, carrying charcoal, clothes and comestibles, which was just as well really, for the exigencies of steepness and altitude made carrying even a day-pack tiring after seven hours. It was thus somewhat mortifying when toiling along in state-of-the-art climbing boots and gore tex kit, carrying only light packs, to be overtaken at great speed by welly-booted porters wearing tatty old shorts and t-shirts, carrying enormous packs with effortless ease. For your average Rwenzori expedition the ratio of porters to climbers works out at about two or three to one. We fondly imagined that by hiring some twenty porters we were doing our bit for the local economy, that is, until we happened to bump into a BBC film crew (as you do in the middle of nowhere). The crew – or, more accurately, both of them - were filming a documentary about the Nile, starting here, at its source. Looking at their procession in amazement, we counted no fewer than 45 porters (so now you know why it costs so much to make TV programmes.).

Whatever you read and imagine about the Rwenzoris, you're little prepared for the reality of the place. Take the vegetation for example: in climbing from an altitude of around 2,000m to over 5,000m (around 6,500ft to 16,500ft) you experience a wide variety of flora, much of it passing strange. It resembles the botany of East African mountains but is much more luxuriant, due to the Rwenzoris' higher rainfall. Once you leave the village shambas fringing the Park, with their crops of cassava, bananas and millet, you ascend through montane forests of Podocarps, Cyanthea (a giant tree fern) and Hibiscus. There's even the familiar sight of *Pteridium aquilinum* - only it's bigger than bad old British bracken. But once you reach 2,500 metres (8,500ft) the 'Lost World' suddenly and bizarrely presents you with - of all things - bamboo groves. You almost expect to see giant pandas shyly chewing on bamboo stems. As if this China syndrome wasn't enough, a bit further up you find yourself - like a Liliputian - walking amongst a giant forest of tree heather (*Philippia johnstonii*). I was used to the Scottish stuff, but this African heather was over four metres tall (Robert Burns eat yer heart oot).

Further up the mountains it's not only the heather that's huge: there are giant spiky lobelias (*L. bequaertii*), and groundsels of tree-like proportions (*Senecio ericirosenii*). Often the trees and shrubs are festooned with masses of *Usnea* (Old Man's Beard) - a pale grey-green lichen, lending a kind of Lord of the Rings enchantment to the forest. Forgetting the pandas now, you almost expect to meet Frodo and Sam along the trail. Even an Ent or two wouldn't surprise you much. It's not all bizarre botany though: stunning purple orchids and delicious golden swathes of everlasting flowers were just two out of many glorious - but more conventional – flowers encountered along the way.

It's only when you're toiling up and down the mountain slopes that you realise just how steep they really are. For example, looking at the person ahead of you often involved eyeballing their boots. But if going uphill was a struggle - holding on to tree roots, pulling yourself up on branches, even negotiating the occasional dodgily-constructed tree branch 'ladder' - then descending was even more hairy. At one point, as the path followed a near vertical burn downhill, our head guide

Daniel became unusually animated, cautioning us to keep well to one side. Asked later why that was, he announced airily that someone 'dieded' there two years ago. "*A porter?*" I enquired. "*No, a tourist*," came the reply. Apparently once you slide into that part of the slippery stream, it's a one-way cascade to the hereafter…

As the days went by, the rapport between our group and the Ugandans grew ever stronger. The best ice-breaker of all was James' frisbee. At Bijuku hut he and Scott initiated our porters into the fine art of touch frisbee. After a while things developed to the point where the mzungus decided to take on the Africans. Bad mistake. What little they possessed in technique, they more than compensated for in stamina. A few minutes into the game, we were totally exhausted and outclassed - clutching our sides, gasping for breath and unable to move. They, on the other hand, ran, dived and generally skipped about like professionals. The only honourable thing to do - we decided - was to give in gracefully, let them organise their own teams, and stick to Travel Scrabble instead. And so the expedition settled down to a kind of evening routine: the Ugandans keeping the camp entertained and amused with frisbee skills; the muzungus settling down to play games of Scrabble. Some of the later Scrabble marathons were so lengthy that we used up head torch batteries by the packet (we blamed the altitude for our lethargy of course). At the end of the expedition, we considered it right and proper to present the frisbee to the 'best team' in a fitting and solemn ceremony: after all, what good was it to us 'also-rans' now?

As summit day approached, we all found ourselves suffering to a greater or lesser degree from the effects of altitude. The dodgy side of mountain climbing is manifest in Acute Mountain Sickness - or AMS - best kept at bay by gradual acclimatisation and lots of drinking (that would be water, unfortunately). After several days of ascending gradually, the time came at last to attempt the summit bid. This moment had been rather hanging over us because most of the party had never been this high before; few had used crampons and rope; and most were suffering from altitude headaches. Added to this some worries about possible crevasses and you had a sure-fire recipe for concern. A cursory crash course in mountain craft the afternoon before summit day did nothing to allay the group's nervousness. So it was a fairly subdued party in the event that awoke (or more accurately arose) at 4am on St Valentine's Day, to attempt Margherita Peak, (5,109m/16,761ft) the highest part of Mt Stanley in the Rwenzoris and the third highest in Africa (after Mounts Kilimanjaro and Kenya). In the Duke of Abruzzi's day, Elena glacier stretched several hundred feet lower than it does now and at one time Elena Hut (the highest hut) nestled close to the white glacier's bosom. This made climbing easier, because all you had to do was stumble out of the door, strap your crampons on, and off you went. But now the situation demands an hour's scrambling over disorientating rocks before you actually reach the foot of the glacier itself. In the pitch dark, with only head-torches to aid us, this was a bit of a nightmare to say the least. Eventually we sorted ourselves out, roped up and started to plod ponderously upwards, pausing for breath on the glacier every few paces. When the daylight appeared, limited visibility from the swirling mists only served to add to the general feeling of gloom.

After five hours toiling up the glacier, most of us could only flop down onto the small saddle of snow joining Uganda to Congo. Here the view now dropped suddenly and dramatically to where - thousands of feet below - the indistinct green haziness of the Congo could dimly be observed. Here also was the point where – until recently – most expeditions stopped and turned back, just 50 metres (170ft) from the summit proper. For this was the Rwenzoris' answer to the 'Hilary Step', a 15 metre sheer face of rock necessitating some technical climbing. Thanks to our intrepid guide Daniel and a length of fixed rope we scraped and clinked our way up this final obstacle - our crampons, our breathing and our humour wearing ever thinner - until at last we cleared the cliff, scrambled round a further rocky outcrop, on to a short stretch of steep ice and finally inched up to the very top itself: a room-sized platform of snow, surrounded by the view of a lifetime.

All around us appeared spectacular glimpses of sheer rock speckled with snow and ice, while far below, glimpses of lush greenery beckoned like a distant African Eden. A sea of angry jagged peaks surrounded the security of our little crow's nest. All worries about crevasses, weather and altitude were forgotten now, as a general wave of euphoria swept through the group. Here we were, a few foolish mzungu, on a natural 'high', defying the planet's gravitational pull: never mind the Mountains of the Moon, this felt more like being on the moon itself. There was no doubt about it: all that toil, all that effort, all that breathlessness had been worth it for the rewards of our Rwenzori rendezvous...

Suddenly the mist swirled round, obscuring the view and dispelling our elation. "*Can we leave now?*" said a small voice from the group. The spell was broken: it was time to go down.

The other expedition members comprised James Ackworth, Scott Geller, Krystyna Krassowska (KK) Matt and Claire Larkin, Miles McCarthy, and Justin Waller. KK – the organiser and expedition leader – is Founder and Outdoor Leadership Educator for idGuides in Indonesia.

Rwenzori

8

Supersize Mount McKinley (2005)

A proving ground for would-be Everest climbers, McKinley is an unforgiving place with a reputation for not suffering fools gladly. Towards the end of our expedition, hubris almost turned to nemesis...

Wearily, I trudged through the soft yielding snow. I was slavishly following the rope that bound me to my fellow mountaineers like an umbilical cord, mesmerised by its hypnotic snake-like passage ever onwards and upwards. This was only Day three of the climb, and already the effects of altitude were beginning to take their toll. "*Why are you climbing McKinley?*" friends asked me before the expedition. "*Because it's there,*" I half-jokingly replied. "*Why the hell are you climbing McKinley?*" I now asked myself. "*God knows,*" I replied indifferently, longing for a break, a rest stop, just a few minutes of respite from the pain of ascending and the need for pressure breathing.

However you define it, McKinley is a unique, supersize mountain. It's the icy jewel in Alaska's frozen crown: at 6,193m (20,320 ft), the tallest place you can reach in north America. In continental terms its height is exceeded only by Aconcagua (South America) and Everest (Asia). Climbers differ in their opinions of its relative height from a 'thin air' point of view. All of the world's other peaks over 20,000ft lie in a relatively narrow band between 32° south and 43°north of the equator, so McKinley presents an oddity, lying as it does in the far north (63° north) less than two hundred miles or 3° from the Arctic Circle. Since the earth's spin creates a thicker mantle of air at the equator and an increasingly thinner coating towards the poles, McKinley's relative height (from the barometric pressure perspective) is thus nearer 7,500m than 6,193m. Hence the need for pressure breathing.

The first part of every climbers' journey to McKinley's Base Camp is an exciting half-hour flight from Talkitna airstrip, which takes off on wheels and tarmac, squeezes precariously through a narrow notch in the foothills (called - appropriately - 'one-shot pass') and lands on skis and snow some way up the forty five mile long Kahiltna glacier. "*Welcome to Kahiltna*

International Airport!" muttered a weary climber waiting to escape the mountain, a haunted, browbeaten look of defeat on his grim bearded face. I tried not to think about failure, or the likelihood of 100mph winds and -40°C temperatures and I tried even more not to dwell on the fact that for the next three weeks we would be seeing no greenery, no animals, no home cooking and no proper toilets…

The granite massif called Denali (in Athabascan meaning 'the Great One') is truly one of the world's most magnificent mountains. It's synonymous with Alaska: the 'Great Land'; land of the midnight sun; a land mass spanning four time zones; land a fifth of the area of the 'lower 48' States. Because of its climate, half of this 'Great Land' is treeless, much of it comprising unbroken tundra. South of that lies an endless green expanse of taiga forest (spruce, with birch, aspen and willow). McKinley itself lies roughly equidistant from Anchorage and Fairbanks – Alaska's two main centres of population. (Juneau – the unlikely State capital – is a much smaller town situated in Alaska's southern 'pan-handle'). The shrewd Americans bought Alaska from the Russians in 1867 for $7.2M. Although many thought that buying this piece of real estate - (some nicknamed it 'Walrussia': others 'Icebergia') - was a waste of money, cynicism turned to schadenfreude when oil was discovered at Alaska's North Slope in 1968. The rest – as they say – is history. Enter economic boom time, the 'Uncle Sam' way of life, and, thirty seven years later, Anchorage is like any other US city: a monument to excess (too many cars, too much fast food and too much obesity).

Meanwhile, back at 3,400m (11,000ft) there was a distinct lack of conspicuous consumption. Having dragged our sorry backsides (not to mention 60lb packs and 30lb sledges) up to Camp One, the twelve of us (nine climbers and three guides) were evolving an end-of-day expedition routine which consisted of putting up tents, digging out a mess/cooking area and sorting out personal kit. This 'climb high, sleep low' approach was called 'acclimatisation' by our guides Ryan, Bill and Dave. We just called it 'sodding hard work'.

Because McKinley rises abruptly from its low level tundra setting, the elevation gain from base to summit (nearly 5,500m/18,000ft) is unsurpassed anywhere in the world, whilst the height gain from Base Camp to summit (13,000ft – nearly 4,000m) is a full 1,000ft greater than the Everest equivalent (29,000ft – 17,000ft). This in itself is an acclimatisation challenge. But whilst on Everest the Sherpas carry all your stuff, here on McKinley, we were the porters. Add to that challenge the lurking dangers of crevasses, avalanches and rock falls, not to mention flash freezing and human error, and Denali offers what amounts to the second most difficult of the seven continental summits. Indeed, it's often used as a testing/training ground for would-be

Everest summiteers.

Since it rises so abruptly from nearly sea level, McKinley effectively creates its own climate. Barometric and weather changes tend to be rapid and severe (as we discovered at Camp One when nocturnal temperatures suddenly dropped to -25°C). This results in lots of frost inside the tent in the morning, frozen water bottles (or worse – frozen pee bottles) if left outside sleeping bags during the night; and parky extremities to boot (and that's just one's feet). That was the night we received an unexpected visitor in the form of 'Crapt'n' Oats': a disorientated, half-frozen sparrow who hopped into our tent, desperately seeking food and shelter. Unfortunately, our panicky visitor's disconcerting habit of perching on our heads, plus its dismal and palpable lack of tent toilet training, led to an inevitable 'big brother' style eviction. We never did discover what happened to our uninvited avian guest but I sadly suspect that the mountain ravens were a little less ravenous the next morning.

For most hopefuls, the normal Denali climbing season is mid-May to mid-July: early enough to avoid crevasse cul-de-sacs and avalanche tumbles, but late enough for temperatures to be bearable. If you're brave enough (or barking enough), Denali can also be climbed during the winter. The first such summit attempt was described graphically in a book called, simply, 'Minus 148' (I'll leave the rest to your imagination…). Each year on average, of the thousand or so people attempting this standard route annually, only about half are successful, around a hundred acquire altitude sickness or frostbite and twelve have to be rescued (over forty people have died on this route).

Roping up in teams of four became a ritual whenever we moved outside camps, whether to 'cache' supplies and return, move up to a new camp, or 'back carry' (descend to collect a previous cache). Such roping up was a necessity, not a luxury. In ascending to Camp Two we were struck by the ever-present threat of crevasses. Sometimes it was the sinister boom of hollow ice beneath one's feet: at other times one could actually view unfathomable depths: sinister holes, chutes and cracks into a dark-blue icy abyss. Crevasses were categorised by our guides as 'ankle-biters', 'bottom-catchers', 'body-snatchers' or 'team-swallowers'. Our team commands ("*zero!*" and "*go!*") served well when a roped member encountered problems (usually temperature regulation or dehydration). On one occasion though, the 'zero!' command was in response to my having a close encounter with a bottom-catcher (very embarrassing, but at least it wasn't a team-swallower). Tragically, over the years, many careless (or less fortunate) Denali climbers have been seduced, swallowed up and entombed within the clutter of crevasses that litter the glaciers that drape the limbs of this frigid femme fatale.

By day six we were all developing well as a team: early morning starts meant that we tended to beat other groups to the best tent pitch spots (i.e. where someone else had laboured to build the ice-block walls essential to keep off winds that could easily exceed 50 mph). As our confidence increased, so we became increasingly sure that the summit prize would inevitably be ours for the taking. And by the time we reached Camp Three at 4,300m (14,000ft), we reckoned on a simple conquering of Denali within the next few days.

Big mistake. The Great One had her own agenda. Away went the clear blue skies and still conditions. Spectacular lenticular clouds hovered over Denali and her near neighbours Mt Foraker and Mt Hunter. Sinister clouds appeared overhead, associated with even more sinister vapour trails that arched menacingly over our tents like ever-changing wraiths, spooks and ghosts. "*Dracula clouds*" the guides called them. "*Forget summitting while the lentics last,*" they said, "*the winds up there are stormy enough to blow you right off the mountainside.*" And thus our confinement began, as we were forced to stay on at Camp Three. And on.

And on. And on. Several books and one giant sandcastle (*alright then – snowcastle*) later, we were ready to get our tails up to the high camp – Camp Four – at 5,200m (17,200 ft) Boy, were we ready. But it was not to be. At least not for a while…

McKinley was summited only as recently as 1913. Before that an attempt by the Duke of Arbruzzi (of Rwenzoris fame) in 1897 reached 5,500m (18,000ft). In 1906, a great hoax was perpetrated when a certain Dr Cook claimed the summit prize. In fact he only reached a minor peak and although the media hailed him as a conquering hero at the time, he was later found out, discredited, vilified and eventually expelled from the Explorers Club.

A legendary summit attempt was made in 1910 by the famous Sourdough Expedition. What started as a whiskey-fuelled bet in a Fairbanks saloon, developed into a courageous mountaineering epic: one of the most noteworthy McKinley expeditions of all time. Carrying a heavy spruce pole, and a 6ft by 12ft US Flag, unacclimatised to altitude and with only basic equipment, two of the four-man party carried the pole to McKinley's second highest summit, in the process climbing and descending 2,400m (8,000ft) in just 18 hours. To record the event they carried a $5 camera. Following the Dr Cook debacle, many cynics rubbished the Sourdough's summit claim. But when - in 1913 - one Walter Harper, climbing towards the south summit, spied on the top of the north peak, *a flagpole of all things*, the Sourdough truth was finally verified - an intrepid feat by brave men who, unfortunately, summited the lower north peak rather than the slightly higher south peak: the true summit of Mt McKinley.

It was left to an English-born missionary – Hudson Stuck, Archdeacon of the Yukon - to claim that prize. Stuck preferred to call the mountain Denali. "*I would rather climb that mountain than discover the richest gold mine in Alaska*" he wrote. On June 7th 1913, his party finally made it. His diary entry read "*.... we shook hands all round and a brief prayer of thanksgiving to Almighty God was said, that He had granted us our heart's desire and brought us safely to the top of His great mountain.*"

Meanwhile, back at Camp Three, after seven days socked-in at 4,300m (14,000ft), just as we were beginning to harbour serious doubts about getting any higher, our own miracle materialised: a weather window sufficient to climb to the final Top Camp at 5,200m (17,2000ft). Reaching this Camp involved some tricky technical work jumaring[1] 215m (700ft) up a fixed rope on a 40° headwall, then belaying into karabiners attached to secure removable aluminium pickets. Eventually we made it along a knife-edge ridge to the small encampment, pleased to be looking down on Camp Three for a change. But as soon as we arrived there, in a cruel display of deja-vu the Great One experienced another sense-of-humour failure and the weather closed in on us again. Other teams – who had been stuck up at Camp Four for up to two weeks waiting for that elusive summit weather window to appear - were forced to descend due to a shortage of food or fuel, or due to work deadlines looming back in the real world. "*Would the same fate befall us?*" we wondered.

As things turned out, we were lucky - or so we thought. On 14 June - our second day at 17,000ft - the sky cleared and the pent-up demand from frustrated climbers materialised into a small wave of would-be summiteers starting to edge up the last thousand metres. But something - some seventh sense - made our guides hesitate and then break the news to us that we were not in fact going to be leaving camp that day. We were all gutted. Would this mean having to go home empty handed?

In the event, not ascending that day was a very wise move. Virtually all of the climbers who set off that morning had to retreat from the relentless and deadly winds that later whipped up into a human heat-seeking wind-chill weapon, efficient and deadly. Unfortunately, two Japanese climbers had to be helped down from 5,800m (19,000ft) after succumbing to the extreme cold.

By this time it was 'now or never' for us. Having spent months of preparation and three weeks of hard climbing to reach this point, we knew that if tomorrow's conditions were not sufficiently good it would be game over, descend, down, and out. That night we tried to sleep: tried not to think of defeat.

---

[1]A technique used to ascend a rope using a hand-held device.

The next morning we awoke to the marvel of a clear day. Having finally subdued our restless summit fever and humbled our impatient egos, Denali the Great One decided at last to give us her blessing: ten hours of unbroken summit weather. No one could have asked for a better present. Seven hours later, at 2.25 p.m. on 15 June, we had the roof of north America to ourselves. Denali held us close to her snowy white bosom. Briefly, she smiled on us….

And at that instant - as it had at the start of this extraordinary adventure - that nagging, imperative question slipped into my mind again. "*Why climb McKinley?*" This time I knew. Only now was it clear to me that simply being here was enough; simply being here was the answer. It was the question itself that was non-sense.

"*Thank you Denali.*" I breathed, before finally turning to descend.

Now, memo number one to self: most accidents happen on the descent. Be bloody careful, Ogilvie.

Memo number two to self: what was that roadhouse pub that the guides recommended for post-climb celebrations? Oh yes, Dick's Half Inn (liquor at the front: poker at the rear). Now, there was both a question and an answer that *did* make perfect sense...for once!

During the Denali climb I shared tent space with Nick Robertson and Alistair Sutcliffe. Since then Al has become a lifelong friend and climbing inspiration. He and his wife Claire have made me welcome at their Whitby home on many occasions. In 2010 Al suffered a massive brain haemorrhage. The doctors told Claire to say her last goodbyes as he wouldn't survive the night, but he did, and his subsequent book '*The Hardest Climb*' recounts how he became the first person to summit the highest mountain on each of the seven continents at the first attempt (which probably makes me the second person!)

Mount McKinley

Everest

Everest

9

The Everest experience - staring down on stars (2007)

Foreword – Sir Chris Bonington CBE

To base camp trekkers and summiteers alike, Everest is a powerful beacon, touching all those who make the pilgrimage to her remote Himalayan sanctuary. Revered by the Sherpa people as mother goddess of the world, Sagamatha exerts a powerful - almost a spiritual - hold on those who chase their dream of standing 'close to heaven'. Enduring symbol of striving and human endeavour, Chomolungma exerts a profound and lasting impact on the lives of those who make that pilgrimage, fulfilling a deep need and bestowing her abundant grace.

Today, developed countries are all too used to gain: materialism and wealth for example, but western culture is equally aware of losing something as society becomes increasingly removed from the harsher realities of life. Our cosseted existence - insulated from the physical challenges that most human beings endure of necessity - is leading inexorably to a decrease in some intangibles: physical challenge, self-esteem, even a lack of spirituality.

The experience of visiting and climbing Everest puts something back. It allows us to chase a majestic dream, yes, but it requires more than a vision to see it through: it also requires fortitude to conquer fears and a determination to prevail through many hardships. Not only is climbing Everest a physical marathon, it's also a mental and psychological one. Summiteers are tested – in a few cases tragically to destruction - and for many the dream is thwarted by all sorts of reasons – dismal weather, poor health, 'bad karma'. But for those lucky few - around two thousand to date - who have stood on the roof of the world, Everest imparts a new and deeper outlook on life: a unique and privileged insight into ourselves and – with luck – a greater understanding of our fellow human beings.

Climbing mountains is not about summiting for vainglorious or egotistical reasons. It's not even about summiting to assuage summit fever. Too many have paid the ultimate price for those reasons, or have walked past people in trouble perhaps abandoning them to death in their desperation to reach the summit. Whether you succeed in getting to the top or not, what is important is being in the experience, being compassionate and aware of the people around you. Yes, it's wonderful - extra-ordinary if you will - to accomplish your target. But adhering to the dream means climbing Everest for Everest's sake – 'because it's there' as it were, rather than out of a desire to impress. As someone once remarked, "*the summit is such a small piece of the mountain. Most of the beauty and wonders are experienced during the climb and in the way you react to the people around you.*"

In 'staring down on stars' James has captured some of that beauty, some of those wonders. He has helped a deserving charity along the way. And I have no doubt that he has learned much from his experience. I commend his account to you.

Chris Bonington, September 2007

Everest - crashed helicopter and tents with snow covering.

The Everest experience - staring down on stars (2007)

So why 'Staring down on Stars'? Read on to find out…

When someone discovers that you've climbed Mount Everest they usually ask you three questions:-

The first is "*Why did you climb it?*" and whilst it's tempting to give Mallory's famous reply "*Because it's there*", in truth, for me, it just sort of happened. No really, it did! It all started fifteen years ago with a short, unplanned and unexpectedly successful climb of Kilimanjaro (the highest mountain in Africa) which ignited a passion for 'getting high'. From there events gradually evolved into a quest for the 'seven summits' (the highest mountains on each of the world's continents), climbing Aconcagua (South America) in 2000 and McKinley (North America) in 2005. And so – if my dream was going to be fulfilled – it seemed only natural to think about tackling Everest before it was 'too late'. Approaching 50, at a job crossroads and with two months leave to spare, it seemed to me that the mountain gods were gently nudging me in the direction of the Himalaya…

The second question relates to mortality. "*Weren't you afraid of dying?*" I'm often asked, and I'd be lying if I said that such a fear doesn't enter the mind of all those who climb Everest. Nowadays, everyone's heard of the 'death zone' (above 7,600m/25,000 ft) made infamous in 1996 when fifteen people lost their lives (last year the figure was twelve). Until 2004, the statistical odds of not coming down alive were about one in eight. However, those odds include the early pioneering expeditions and although there are always several deaths each year, today's odds are much better than 1 in 10 – and improving steadily. And since the 1996 disaster, weather forecasting accuracy and rescue infrastructure have also improved greatly.

The third question is "*What's it like to stand on top of the world?*" and I'll tell you in a minute, but before I do let's start at the beginning…

Symbol of mental endurance, physical striving and human endeavour, Everest has been the subject of countless books, films and documentaries. Originally called 'Peak XV' by the cartographers, the Nepalese know it as Sagarmatha ('goddess of the sky') whilst the Tibetans call it Chomoloungma ('goddess, mother of the earth'). It was labelled Mount Everest after Sir George Everest, British Surveyor General in India in the mid-19th century and since 1924 it's been the stuff of dreams for small (and not-so-small) boys (and girls). For it was then that two members of a British expedition - Mallory and Irvine - disappeared whilst 'going strong' for the summit. Ten more expeditions, thirteen deaths and nearly thirty years later, the world's ultimate summit still proved to be frustratingly elusive. And then in 1953, Edmund Hillary and Tenzing Norgay became the first to reach the roof of the world, ascending from the Nepalese side (which had eased its restrictions on foreigners at about the same time that Tibet - invaded in 1950 by China - shut its borders). The news reached London just in time for Elizabeth II's coronation. World-famous overnight, Hillary became a hero of the British Empire, whilst Tenzing was hailed as a symbol of national pride not only by Nepal but also by Tibet and India.

Today, most climbers and trekkers start the journey to Everest Base Camp from Lukla airport. At one time a short dirt strip that involved hairy landings, Lukla airstrip is now tarmac, but it's still short and it's still hairy. Although the 'runway' is pitched at a ridiculously steep angle to assist take off, pilots still have to squeeze every inch out of the space available before revving up, letting off the handbrake and immediately disappearing out of sight down the runway towards the abyss below…

But once arriving visitors have overcome their near-death experience of a Lukla landing, their trek through the Himalayas becomes a sheer delight. Gone are the cars and internal combustion engines; gone are the dust and pollution of Kathmandu's air and gone are the crowds and the cacophony. As you gradually adjust to life without vehicles your walk into the Sagarmatha National Park becomes an increasingly delightful blend of sights, sounds and scents. Lush pine and fir forests, interspersed with smallholdings and fields of potatoes, barley and buckwheat, gradually give way to scented rhododendrons, then alpine meadows, juniper scrub, arctic lichens and eventually a sparser, harsher world of snow, rock and ice. Every few kilometres, quaint wooden and stone tea-houses line the path, gaudy signboards inviting visitors to experience their particular hospitality. The friendly greeting 'Namaste' (literally 'I salute the divine within you') is always on the lips of passing porters, sherpas and schoolchildren. This is a trekker's paradise and even if you don't harbour a desire to bag peaks I would urge you to experience the vitality, energy and sheer enjoyment of an organised trek in this Himalayan shangri-la: you won't regret it. But for the climber with a more ambitious agenda whose eye is drawn upwards to majestic sky-scraping mountains framed by swirling clouds - peaks like Ama Dablam, Cho Oyo and Lhotse - the sheer immensity - even impertinence - of undertaking an ascent of the world's highest peak, gradually begins to sink in.

At 3,350m (11,000ft) lies the renowned village of Namche Bazar, gateway to the Khumbu Valley. It's a motley collection of solidly constructed hotels, hostels, guesthouses and shops, each with a brightly painted roof, nestled in a horseshoe-shaped amphitheatre. Somehow Namche's shops are able to stock an amazing assortment of kit for walkers and climbers, some of it recycled from previous expeditions. But it's a sobering thought that all new goods have to be carried on the backs of porters for at least a day (probably several) before reaching this place, which itself is several days' hike (for an acclimatised person, that is) from Base Camp itself. Like many frontiers, Namche is a last bastion of civilisation for sophisticated travellers. Beyond here you can kiss goodbye to en-suite showers and flushing toilets and say hello to one's first glimpse of Mount Everest, twenty six miles distant. Viewed from here it's a small, almost demure triangle of rock and ice, much less impressive than the closer and shapelier outline of Ama Dablam, and it's difficult from this distance to appreciate just how immense a mountain it really is.

Expeditions preparing for the two month 'assault' on Everest have to stock up with literally tons of supplies - food, equipment, oxygen cylinders and other paraphernalia. With roads having disappeared many miles before here, the customary form of transport is the trusty, patient and gentle yak. Adapted to life above 3,000 metres, yaks are used extensively above Namche (they overheat below this altitude) and visiting expeditions provide a welcome source of revenue for the local yak breeders and herders (our expedition alone used over 160 yaks to transport supplies to Base Camp). Some of the yak trains comprised as many as a dozen beasts, adorned with earrings and blankets ('yaccessorised' perhaps?) by their devoted owners and announcing their presence with the sonorous ringing of neck bells. Ever respectful, yaks encountering westerners on a narrow section of the trail would wait, wide-eyed and patient for the trekkers to step aside and clear the path before continuing on their sure-footed way.

Every so often - usually at watersheds, viewpoints and entrances to villages - the trail would pass by various relicts and reminders of Buddhism. Sometimes these comprised onion-shaped stupas or Buddhist shrines, painted gold and white and decorated with the single Buddhist eye (the third eye or eye of wisdom - symbol of enlightenment). At other times there were prayer wheels and bells (water-driven or revolved by the hands of passers-by) tall flag poles and Mani stones (carved rocks or piles of old stone tablets carved with Buddhist mantras). Often such artefacts were adorned with 'wind horses' or prayer flags, brightly coloured in red (representing fire), white (air or cloud), yellow (earth), green (water) and blue (space). Respectful travellers always passed by on the left of such objects and revolved prayer wheels clockwise with the right hand. It was interesting to see how many otherwise agnostic western climbers became almost paranoically reverent (or possibly just superstitious?) in the lead up to the climb itself, going out of their way to 'do the right thing'. These constant reminders of Buddhism were one of the many delights of the trail and an appropriate prelude to the spiritual importance with which many Nepalese people regarded Everest itself (according to Sherpa tradition, Miyo Lungsangma is Chomolongma's resident goddess, mother goddess of the earth).

The Sherpa people are nothing if not superstitious and their beliefs include the notion of bad luck (or *annus horribilis*) years which occur about every decade or so. Knowing nothing of this, it came as a surprise to me when, on visiting a monastery, the Lama or chief monk informed us that 2007 was such a year. In these bad luck years no Sherpa marriages take place and no buildings are constructed. Oh, and by the way, no sensible person would risk their life climbing a momentous mountain, either! The khama went from bad to worse however, when he added that certain ages were also bad luck and, yes - you guessed - it just so happened that mine was one. So double bad luck for me then. At this point I was beginning to have grave doubts about the wisdom of embarking on an Everest escapade in 2007. It was going to need some seriously good khama to counteract all this bad luck.

Happily for me, our expedition immediately embarked upon an intensive programme of holy blessings and monastery visits (including Thame, one of Nepal's oldest Buddhist monasteries). Whilst my fears were not completely assuaged, some holy forehead rubbing plus presents of blessed (kata) scarves and a personalised prayer card were at least some comfort, as was the expedition's Puja ceremony at Base Camp (even though the auspicious date chosen was Friday 13th April!). This is a vital part of any Everest quest in which offerings are placed on an adorned stone altar and the participants - climbers, leaders and sherpas alike - chant, pray, drink, dance and throw blessed rice. It's a typical Buddhist mixture of the reverential and the comical where all the participants end up chucking tsampa (barley flour) at each other and dancing in a tightly-knit semicircle. During the Puja ceremony long streamers of wind horses (always an odd number) are attached to a central flagpole and secured to distant rocks. Alongside these colourful flags flutter nature's own black scraps of cheekiness, the ever-present jackdaw-like choughs. These provide one of the few non-human life forms at altitude, even occasionally visiting the South Col at 8,000m (26,200ft). To the Sherpa people choughs represent the spirits of dead climbers and are therefore treated with great respect (and also treated to food leftovers).

It's supposed to be good luck if one lands on the flagpole during a Puja and I for one, remembering the bad luck concern, was glad when it finally happened ('highly choughed' even!).

At first, Base Camp strikes you as a bleak place – a constantly changing tented village devoid of any vegetation, bordered by the corpses of dead helicopters, with the only fauna being a few birds and visiting yaks. But it is extraordinary how adaptable human beings are and how quickly a place can become 'home from home'. Strange noises - like the gunshot cracking of the ice beneath our tents, or the many avalanches and rock falls from the surrounding slopes - quickly became familiar after a while: almost background noise. This place is a geologist's dream, a landscape under construction. Every year Base Camp becomes obliterated by snow and shifting permafrost. Nothing seems to stay the same for long here except perhaps the mountain tops themselves (although even they are subjected to powerful tectonic forces: Everest grows by a few millimetres each year). So here we were, home from home, thinking nothing of living nearly two thousand feet above the top of the Alps and over three miles above sea level. At the same time we knew that, hidden from sight, the top of Everest was another two miles above us, at getting on for six miles above sea level! Base Camp's reputation as a rubbish tip is happily outdated now. Thanks to the efforts of the Sagarmatha Pollution Control Committee and donations from developed nations, porters are paid to take refuse away to be disposed of properly. This is helped by the fact that many expeditions (ours included) practice environmentally appropriate 'Leave No Trace' principles and practices.

For climbers like us attempting the South Col route, the Khumbu Icefall is an ever-present spectre that hangs over you like the sword of Damocles. Faced by Hilary and Tenzing, this life-threatening obstacle is where the Western Cwm (the world's highest valley) disgorges its immense glacial river of ice towards Base Camp in a chaotic mass of gigantic tottering ice blocks, towers, columns and wedges. Nothing prepares you for the experience of climbing here. Passing like a Lilliputian through this giant jumbled landscape - with sections nicknamed 'the popcorn' and 'the playing field' - makes you supremely aware of your own mortality. Holding your breath (never a good idea in thin air) you hurry past tottering blocks of rotten ice, keeping your fingers crossed that they haven't got your name written on them. In this environment huge icy slabs threaten to fall at random and without warning. At the drop of an ice axe you can become a prime candidate for a so-called 'Darwin Award' – given to people who end their lives in mind-numbingly stupid ways. No climber in their right mind would ordinarily traverse such life-threatening topography, where, at any moment, vast ice behemoths weighing many tons could crush the life out of you.

And yet this is no ordinary climb: negotiating the Khumbu Icefall in the pursuit of altitude and acclimatisation is an inescapable fact of life for all climbers from the Nepalese side, not just once but six or more times. For those Sherpa transporting equipment to higher camps, twice that number of Icefall traverses is not uncommon. An unacclimatised climber will take about nine hours to negotiate the Icefall. By the third time that's down to about five hours – but that's still five hours too long. Although this year we were lucky, in previous years there have been cases of climbers simply disappearing under an icefall collapse, the only sign now being lines of prayer flags to mark their icy graves. And as the spring season advances and the ice warms up, collapses become more commonplace. When Sir Edmund Hillary's expedition achieved the summit over fifty years ago it took weeks and months of painstaking work to negotiate the Khumbu icefall.

Fortunately for would-be summiteers today, there exists a cadre of brave Sherpas whose job it is to keep the spidery thread of fixed lines functioning, the crevasse ladders stable and the rope anchors and pickets secure. These unsung heroes - the 'Icefall Doctors' as they are called - defy death almost daily, risking life and limb to fix collapses and keep the route functioning. We were fortunate: the angel of death left our expedition alone (even avoiding those insouciant Sherpas who took a nonchalant approach to the task of clipping in to fixed lines) but others weren't so lucky in this bad luck year. A Sherpa was killed by falling ice; two Koreans seeking a new route from Camp Two were killed by an avalanche; and – particularly distressing – the legendary Sherpani guide Pemba Dorma[1] fell to her death down the Lhotse face on 21 May. Unnervingly for us, the retrieving of these bodies always seemed to coincide with our ascent of the icefall, a poignant reminder of the dangers inherent in climbing Everest.

Base camp for the early 1950s and 1960s expeditions was about a kilometre distant from its present location and on idle days I sometimes went over there to scavenge for historic artefacts like antique crampons, tent pegs and karabiners. Most of it has been either souvenir hunted or cleaned up by the Sagarmatha Pollution Control Committee, but there were several wooden poles to be seen, roughly hewn on one side and bearing crampon marks on the other - a reminder of the days of when tree trunks were used to cross crevasses rather than today's ubiquitous aluminium ladders. Today there are many such crevasse crossings in and above the Icefall and after some practice with crampons at base camp we became expert (relaxed, even) at crossing ladders lashed together over chasms stretching hundreds of feet below.

---

[1]Pemba Doma Sherpa (1970 - 2007) was the first Nepali female mountaineer to climb Mt. Everest via its north face, the second Nepali woman to summit from both the north and south faces, and one of only six women to have summited Everest twice.

Expeditions climbing the South Col route generally use four camps before the summit. Camp One at the top of the icefall (5,943m/19,500ft - height of Kilimanjaro); Camp Two at the head of the Western Cwm (6,400m /21,000ft - a bit higher than McKinley); Camp Three halfway up the mile long/50 degree Lhotse Face (7,200m/23,500ft - a bit higher than Aconcagua); and Camp Four at the South Col (8,000m/26,3 feet - OK now you're much higher than any mountain peak outside the Himalayas). Most of the camps are less than a Scottish Munro apart (i.e. 914m/3,000ft) and if tackled at Scotland's altitudes would present little challenge. But at high altitudes, often in extreme cold or sometimes (paradoxically) blistering ultraviolet heat, such height gains present enormous difficulties for climbers.

Acclimatisation is everything in this slow motion, pressure breathing, crampon shuffling world and that's one reason why the average Everest expedition is as long as it is. Following the mantra of 'climb high, sleep low' most expeditions are a bit like three separate climbs: first to Camp One, then back to Base Camp; then to Camp Three and back to Base Camp; and finally all the way to the summit. At altitude, each footstep can be a fight for breath and even with the assistance of extra oxygen the effort (about 600 calories an hour to be precise) can be intense during a twelve or more hour day. For us the highest overnight 'sleep' without supplementary oxygen was Camp Three. Here, the top of Everest beckons and all your summit fever instincts tell you to go onwards and upwards. But counter-intuitively the best thing at this point is actually to descend to below Base Camp to rich air, lush vegetation, a comfortable bed and lots of food. So that's what we did and much good it did me, after a bout of food poisoning and consequential 'Kathmandu quickstep' followed by four days of starvation. But at least it worked for the others…

The main months for an Everest expedition are April and May, the drier pre-monsoon season. You expect a two-month expedition to be a physical marathon but it can also develop into a mental and psychological marathon as well: waiting for the right weather; dealing with days of forced inactivity interspersed with bouts of frenzied activity; flapping tents; climbers with 'Khumbu cough' depriving you of sleep; tensions arising between climbers – the stress list is endless. Keeping balanced in your head is a vital component to summit success, the name of the game being physical and mental acclimatisation. Bad weather took its toll on climber patience and expedition equipment (several tents were destroyed during a storm at Camp Two). But with a bit of luck and a lot of determination, you eventually reach the South Col and Camp Four at 8,000m (26,000ft) - launch pad for the summit…

For most westerners, climbing in the Himalayas would be impossible without the help of Sherpas. The Sherpa people migrated from eastern Tibet to Nepal within the last 500 years and most of Nepal's 150,000 Sherpas live in the eastern part of the country. Speaking their own language, which in many ways resembles a dialect of Tibetan, Sherpas were immensely helpful to early Himalayan explorers. Today they are still renowned in the international climbing community for their hardiness, expertise, and experience (some people reckon that, genetically speaking, Sherpas have a greater lung capacity, allowing much better performance at high altitudes). Although the term Sherpa is used to refer to almost any guide or porter hired for mountaineering expeditions in Nepal, Sherpas insist on distinguishing between themselves and general porters, given that they serve more as guides and command higher pay and respect from the community. On May 16th the legendary climber Appa Sherpa summited Mount Everest for the 17th time, breaking his own record for the greatest number of successful ascents. Our summit day climb was sufficiently resourced to enable a ratio of one Sherpa to one climber and I was fortunate indeed to have as my companion Chhewang Nima Sherpa from Khumbu. Some ten years younger than Appa, Chewang had fifteen Everest summits to his name[2]. So as we left Camp Four at 9.30pm on the night of 21st May, it was comforting to know that my personal guide and climbing buddy was almost certainly the most experienced summiteer on the mountain at that moment.

On the morning of 22nd May, after passing the Balcony, the South Summit and the Hillary Step, and as the summit draws nearer, it's time to return to those three questions again. I've answered "*Why climb it?*" and "*Weren't you afraid of dying?*" The third question usually asked is "*What's it like to stand on top of the world?*" and in truth not many people can answer that today: many fewer than two thousand[3]. It's too trivial to say that the experience of gazing down on creation is simply incomparable, matchless, unique. For most climbers it's a life-changing experience: after you've stood up there, nothing is ever the same. Although one of our guides once said jokingly of the 8,850m/29,028ft summit 'you're in outer space', it certainly feels like it when you can clearly see the curvature of the earth below you. You're at jetstream altitude, looking down from Everest's pinnacle on giant peaks like Makalu, standing not far off the cruising height of the plane that took you to Kathmandu. Well acclimatised by now, you can remove your oxygen mask for a while and - even with 1/3rd of the oxygen found at sea level - appreciate some precious,

---

[2]Chhewang Nima went on to make that a total of nineteen times but was tragically killed by an avalanche near the summit of Mount Baruntse in 2010.

[3] Now- in 2015 - nearer four thousand.

all-too-brief moments gazing at the world spread out below you.

In those priceless moments of immortality, for all of us standing on Everest's summit that day, we had become, at long last, children of Miyo Lungsangma, mother goddess of the earth and the sky...

But as a final postscript, one of the most extraordinary memories of summit day for me was during the long, long hours before dawn when I first became aware of the horizon actually being below me and noticing with a tremendous sense of wonderment the twinkling of stars shining there. When you're used to seeing constellations in the firmament above you, the surprise of staring down on stars is simply breath-taking: a powerful illustration of just how high the mountain is and just how high one has climbed. And for me, it was also a metaphor for all those human luminaries of the climbing world: stars like Hillary, Tenzing, Venables and the early pioneering giants who had trodden this path before, blazing a trail to the summit for lesser mortals like me to follow. And finally, they symbolised those other human stars there that day, the Sherpa guides and climbers of all nationalities above and below me at that moment, each daring to live their dream, each daring to overcome their fears and each daring to triumph.

Yes, staring down on stars: that to me was the major, magical, miraculous and ultimately defining 'Everest experience'.

One of my fellow Brits on this international expedition - Amy Beeton - is the only British woman alive to have attempted K2 and one of only a handful of British women to have reached the summit of Everest. We still keep the memories of Everest alive with occasional hill-walks in Scotland and the Lake District.

Everest

Chhewang Nima Sherpa

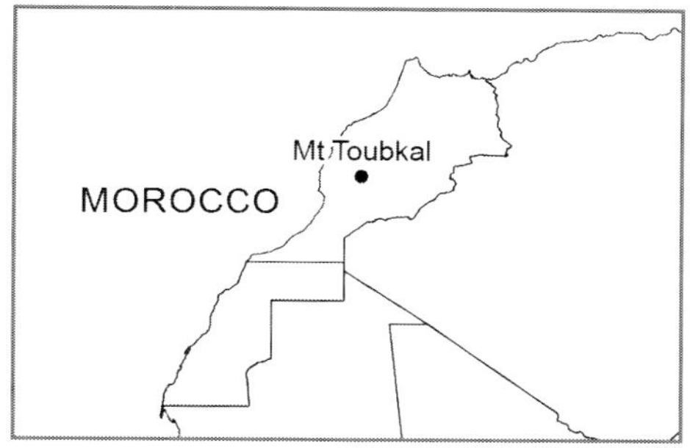

10

Toubkal Trouble (2008)

In the summer you can practically climb Morocco's Mt Toubkal in shorts and a T shirt, but in the winter of 2008 Imogen and I experienced the worst storm I have ever encountered in the mountains…

"*Easy peasy, lemon squeezy,*" exhorted Lahsen, our Berber guide. We hesitated, unconvinced, angels fearing to tread. Up ahead, what should have been a gently sloping path was in fact a gently flowing ribbon of treacherous ice. Beneath it the snowy slope plunged vertiginously towards a raging cataract at the foot of the valley far below. Falling down there would definitely spoil your whole day: no, actually your whole new year. This was day one of our Marrakech climb and already we wished that we'd taken our crampons and ice axes with us instead of letting the porters carry them ahead to the refuge hut…

"*No worries, chicken curries,*" urged Lahsen again, grinning at the eight clients of mixed age, mixed gender and mixed ability who had signed up for the Exodus Mt. Toubkal winter ascent. After some hesitation - and trying not to look downwards - we inched our way gently past the icy obstacle to regain the security of terra firma, at which point - like our route - things started to look up. Ahead, framed by a vivid blue sky and bathed in glorious African sunshine beckoned the snowy peaks of the High Atlas, and in particular Jebel Toubkal, at 4,167m (13,671ft) the highest peak in North Africa and our ultimate goal. The trek, which took us southwards from Imlil (end of the road by Landrover from Marrakech) to the Neltner Refuge, was a sheer delight. Oh, apart from the altitude, that is.

As we plodded the 1,200m (4,000ft) steadily upwards from Imlil most of the group contemplated that there were worse ways to spend the first day of 2008. I however reflected that that miniature of whisky I'd brought from Scotland to celebrate Hogmanay still languished in my kit bag (along with my ice axe and crampons), redundant after our 9pm Ne'ers eve lights out. "*Oh well,*" I cogitated, huffing and puffing my way upwards, "*hopefully it will come in useful to toast a successful Toubkal ascent*".

Ahead of me on the trail, and definitely not huffing and puffing, stormed daughter Imogen – inspiration for this trip. She it was who suggested a gap-year brief taste of adventure in north Africa, roughing it for a few days as a prelude to her forthcoming Bolivian trip. The Exodus blurb described this trip as "*Tough. A strenuous winter trek to an area of outstanding scenic and cultural interest. It is likely that there will be large patches of snow to traverse, therefore ice axe and crampons are a necessity on all departures. There are some steep sections and some areas with a high level of exposure.*" Being fresh to winter climbing Imogen would find this a good learning curve. Being fresh from my Everest ascent nine months before, I would find it a breeze: but beware hubris preceding nemesis. I it was who five hours later at the Neltner Refuge, spectacularly threw up from the effects of attitude. The rest of the group suffered variously from headaches, nausea and lethargy. Imy just took it all in her stride.

Our 'home from home' for the next few days, Neltner consisted of a couple of solidly constructed two-storey buildings divided into sleeping dormitories, eating areas, ablution areas and communal areas. Although substantial in size (our 'hut' boasted several dorms) when full of climbers coming and going it seemed somehow much smaller. When the sun disappeared behind the jagged ridge high above us it was like someone turning off a heater. Shortly afterwards there was a gentle jostling amongst climbers and guides for the best seats beside the wood-fuelled stove in the corner of the cosy 'living room'.

At supper that evening most of our group sat examining their food rather than eating it. Still suffering, we had all hoped for a gentle acclimatisation hike the following day. So when Yahya – our Berber leader – announced that we were going to climb Mt Toubkal, we were both excited and apprehensive. How would an additional 900m (3,000ft) of altitude affect us, not to mention the steeper terrain and winter conditions? Happily, that afternoon, some of the group members' worries about technical inexperience were allayed following an ice-axe arrest practice session on the slopes above the hut. It was a sleepless bunch on the whole who, at 6.30 the next morning, gazed unhungrily at their porridge and thought about the ascent ahead.

As it happened, deciding to climb Mt Toubkal that day was a very good call. Although windy, the sky was cloudless and visibility was good. Gaining ground steadily up the couloir above the refuge, we observed the roseate tints of sunrise spreading their pink glow down the surrounding peaks, chasing away early morning shadows - and climbers' apprehensions. Reaching the rock strewn ridge at 3,800 m (12,500ft) we could begin to make out the snowcapped Anti Atlas range sparkling in the sun some hundred kilometres distant. Four hours after setting out from the Neltner, after a weary trudge up the rocky ridge, we spied the metal pyramidal 'hat' which marked the top of north Africa. Jebel Toubkal was within our grasp!

With Lahsen held back to help slower members of the group, Imy stormed ahead, first to touch the 4,167m (13,671ft) top. And what wonderful views greeted us in all directions! To the south west stood the imposing Ouanoukrim (4,088m/13,400ft), north Africa's second highest peak; to the north, Imlil village, its green vegetation a sharp contrast to Toubkal's Windsor & Newton tints of ochre, burnt umber and sienna. Further north towards Marrakech stretched a fleecy blanket of low-lying cloud obscuring everything else. From our eyrie, that distant fluffy blanket looked benign – gentle, even – but we weren't to know that it was to signal a dramatic change in the weather – and the fortunes of our Exodus expedition. Later, basking in the early afternoon sun outside Neltner, sipping a celebratory tot of whisky and watching the graceful soaring of a Lammergeyer (bearded vulture) just above our heads, we remained blissfully unaware of just how much our luck was about to change…

As evening advanced, the wind picked up, rattling the shutters of the shelter and sending a fine cascade of spindrift through the ill-fitting casements. By now well acclimatised to the altitude, I for one was looking forward to seeing the views from Ouanoukrim, widely regarded as being even more spectacular than those from Toubkal. But venturing out of Neltner the next morning required us to don all the harsh weather gear we possessed. Overhead, wraiths of cloud hurtled across the sky like frenzied phantasms – an ominous sign. Chased up the snowy valley by the wind at our backs we were unable to discern the track which was clearly visible the day before, blissfully ignorant of just how 'gnarly' the conditions were becoming. Reaching the Col at 3,800m (10,100ft) it was by now obvious to all that the show was over. Nobody would be going higher towards the 4,088m (13,400ft) summit: they would simply be scooped off the exposed ridge by the gale and hurled onto the rocks far below. As we turned to head back down, our troubles were only just beginning: all eyewear - glasses and goggles - froze in an instant, covered with a layer of frost impossible to remove. Yet not to clear it meant zero visibility. Taking off the plastic or glass protection from in front of one's eyes also resulted in zero visibility as a hail of stinging spindrift assaulted one's face like gunshot volleys. By now resembling a sightless procession - the blind leading the blind - we fumbled our way downwards, taking a short cut through the thigh-high snow, desperate to obtain shelter and regroup. Veteran of many mountain climbs, I have to say that I was definitely finding the conditions becoming rather too hairy. Eventually, out of the wind in the protection of a large rock, we shook our frozen extremities to try and stimulate circulation and breathed a collective sigh of relief. Imy's insouciant understatement at that point? "*Good winter-climbing experience, eh?!*"

Disappointed not to have summited Ouanoukrim, we were nevertheless eight relieved climbers who returned four hours later to the safety and shelter of Neltner. "*Maybe tomorrow?*" we asked Yahya optimistically. He smiled and shrugged. "*Tomorrow we go down. It takes ten hours to climb Ouanoukrim and return to Imlil. Under these conditions it would take longer*". So we reluctantly packed our bags that evening, ready to return to civilisation. But unbeknown to us, our Toubkal trouble was just about to become double trouble…

By the next morning the wind had increased to gale force. Spindrift was flying everywhere; wind-chill temperatures were well into the minuses and visibility down to only a few metres. However, perhaps encouraged by another team of relatively inexperienced climbers who ventured into the teeth of the gale like a Captain Oates collective, we kitted up as best we could and followed them out into the tempest. Practically blown backwards by the wind, we had to fight our way just to progress downhill. But every few seconds Lahsen stopped, looking back over his shoulder to see if the group was still following. Already it was starting to feel like a fight for survival and by now we had only ventured 300 metres. A rapid consultation was held - shouted above the shrieking of the gale - and sensibly, the decision was taken to turn back. What seemed like ages later we pushed open the refuge door and collapsed inside. "*Better to lose a flight than lose a life,*" we all agreed. Nearly three hours later, the group that had bravely set out earlier stumbled back to Neltner like the walking wounded, broken and defeated, some in tears. We were relieved that they had seen sense and turned back: any longer in those conditions and things might have been much worse…

After what can only be described as a simply gruelling afternoon and evening playing cards and Scrabble, and having finally secured some flapping shutters that had kept us awake, a good night's sleep was finally had by all. The next day, clear blue skies heralded the dawn of a beautiful Moroccan day. The rising sun reflected scintillas of light like jewels in the snowy crown of the Atlas. Gone with the wind were the struggles and the tears. A new dawn brought a new day – a day of hope and anticipation. All that remained for us to do was to descend gently and unhurriedly towards lunch in Imlil.

Easy peasy, lemon squeezy.

Toubkal

Elbrus

11

Angels on Elbrus (2008)

In climbing Europe's highest mountain it was a case of experiencing angels in more than one sense of the word…

I reckon I have a travel guardian angel. That's because my penchant for leaving deadlines until the last minute always seems to pay off, usually to the dismay and consternation of travelling companions. After learning lessons the hard way, those who know about my sloppy timekeeping invariably decide to take charge, insisting on getting them (and me) to the airport or station in very good time. Those unfamiliar with my blatant disregard for contingency and my stubborn refusal to believe that anything can possibly go wrong, usually end their journey minus the ends of their finger nails, vowing at best to set off much earlier, at worst never to travel with me again.

So when - after landing at Heathrow's Terminal 5, collecting my climbing gear, finding the train to Terminal 2 and making a mad (and lengthy) trolley dash to Aeroflot check-in - the representative told me that all seats were taken, I realised with a brutal shock that my luck had finally run out. My travel guardian angel - who had faithfully served my feckless insouciance over the years with unswerving fortitude - had finally disappeared, abandoning me as a bad job. OK the trip dossier did say 'allow at least three hours prior to departure' and here I was arriving with half that time to spare, but as a Terminal 5 virgin how was I to know that the transfer to Terminal 2 would take so long?

With no seats left, all my cherished dreams of adding another scalp to my collection of continental summits evaporated in an instant. I stood at the check-in desk feeling helpless and stupid and imagining the reaction from friends and colleagues. Knowing my lucky laid-back approach to deadlines, they would probably fall about laughing; enjoying the Schadenfreude they had anticipated for so long.

But just as I was about to turn away in despair the chap at the counter was approached by another Aeroflot representative and a rapid conversation ensued in Russian. "*Just a moment,*" he said to me in faultless English, "*It seems that a passenger has had to cancel and is no longer travelling.*" My despair picked itself off the floor and I dared to hope that I might actually join the scheduled expedition after all. Anxious moments ensued whilst he studied his computer screen intently. I waited, each second taking an hour off my life: this time it was my turn to do the nail biting. Two Russian students turned up at the check-in desk complete with trolleys and luggage. "*There are no more seats,*" he said to them dismissively, "*You will have to take a later flight.*" Which was a joke because there were no more Aeroflot flights that day.

After what seemed like an eternity the man turned to me. "*OK, here is your ticket. Enjoy the flight.*" I could have kissed him (fortunately I didn't as this might have caused him to reverse his decision). So my faithful travel guardian angel hadn't abandoned me after all. As if further proof were needed, my angel decided that no ordinary flight would do. No, my ticket had to be in Business Class. Now that was a complete bummer because I had planned to spend the overnight flight catching up on some much-needed sleep and now I was going to have to spend it eating caviar and drinking champagne. Life could be so unfair sometimes…

The highest mountain in Europe, Elbrus lies in Russia. Why this is so I have never fully understood but there it is: if you want to bag the Seven Summits - the highest mountains on Earth's seven continents – you have to go to Russia; Mont Blanc simply won't do. Now that's a pity because a) France is much closer and b) it's not on the Foreign Office list of places to avoid. The FCO's tetchiness has something to do with the region's proximity to Georgia and Chechnya rebels. Before flying out, we thought they were being unduly pessimistic until the Russian/ Georgian conflict inconveniently erupted half-way through our expedition, with Georgian raids on South Ossetia and retaliatory Russian bombing raids on Georgia.

Only five miles from the Georgian border, Cheget is a small village lying not far from the foot of Mt Elbrus, the rendezvous for most expeditions. As we approached, our driver pointed excitedly to the nearby mountain and declared "*Cheget, Cheget! - Chicken, Chicken!*" In turn we pointed up and repeated, "*Chicken, Chicken*". Aha, so that was the name of the local mountain. It was only later that I discovered that its proper name was actually Donguz-Orun-Gitche-Cheget-Cara-Bashi or 'the little north black place at the swine place'. Not too many chickens there then.

Cheget has a frontier, bandit-like feel about it. The Queen's English is hardly spoken, the Queen's sterling is completely useless (only roubles will do) and to complete the Wild West experience, horses roam the streets. But it's also a place of contrasts, for the adjoining village of Terskol is one of Russia's premier skiing resorts. Why I divulge this piece of information will become clear shortly…

The Prielbrusye National Park in general and Cheget in particular are ideal places to begin acclimatising to Caucasus altitudes. We started our programme by heading up the Cheget foothills through scented pine forests and alpine meadows. In August the National Park is resplendent with carpets of wild flowers, but as the guidebook puts it, '*It's impossible to permit picking these splendid flowers and to brake harmony of their inflorescences.*' (sic).

During this part of the expedition we enjoyed the company of Sasha, one of our Russian guides. His was an interesting approach to communication: when he met us off the plane at Minerale Vodny ('Mineral Water'), his first words were, "*My English crazy*". We were not to be disappointed. When asked if we could have some water at lunchtime he replied "*You want music turn down?*" and when asked whether we could drink the tap water he replied "*Maybe yes… maybe no.*" No chance of any ambiguity there then. Yet I sensed that Sasha was an intellectual trapped in a mountain guide's body, for one lunchtime he suddenly and bizarrely found his full command of English and talked to me animatedly about a nearby international research station dedicated to studying neutrinos and the existence of dark matter. No really, he did.

Ten million years ago Elbrus was a volcano. Since then it has erupted several times, although today, as the guidebook charmingly puts it, '*magma gets cold in its entrails*'. This is unfortunate since it means that there's really nowhere to have a warm bath on its slopes. As befits Europe's highest mountain, it boasts several names including 'Tall' in Iranian (no surprises for guessing that one), 'Snow Mane' in Georgian and my personal favourite 'Mount of Happiness' in Circassian. Despite the absence of trees on Elbrus' higher slopes, there's also a rather apt forestry connection because the ancients knew the mountain as 'Strobilus' – the Latin for pine cone. Personally I'm surprised that the Russians don't call it 'Giant Breasts' since that's what Elbrus' twin peaks resembled to me (or perhaps it was just my one-track mind?).

Sexual inequality is ubiquitous in Russia. At the hotel, women cleaned the rooms and slaved in the kitchen, turning out simple but usually tasty meals, whilst the men sat around on their behinds putting the world to rights. Having bought a pack of cards in the local market and unwrapping it from its cellophane I was not altogether surprised to find them arranged in the order: ace, king, jack, then queen. Men first, women last. Perhaps that's why one of Elbrus' best kept secrets is that the higher of its twin peaks was first climbed by (whisper it quietly) – a woman! Florence Cranford Grove first summited Elbrus' higher western summit in 1874. Women (and men) were made of sterner stuff in those days. Not for them today's relative luxury of mountain huts and ski lifts. Ah, yes the ski resort issue again... Well I suppose it's difficult not to have ski lifts in a ski resort and this corner of Russia supports a modest but fast growing skiing infrastructure. Climbers are rather schizophrenic about this fact since it can take some of the sweat (and street cred) out of climbing the mountain. Next time you have a conversation with a self-satisfied "*I've stood on the roof of Europe*" climber, nod sagely and ask them if they enjoyed being whisked effortlessly to 3,800m, thereby avoiding having to climb up the first two thirds of the mountain. I recently had a Monty Pythonesque conversation with one such climber that went something like this:

"*What have the Russians ever done for us?*"

"*Well, they built three ski lifts to help climbers up Elbrus.*"

"*Yes, but apart from that, what have they ever done for us?*"

"*Well, they built some huts on the mountain.*"

"*Yes, but apart from that, what have they ever done for us?*"

"*Well, they gave us snowmobile assistance to take our kit from the chairlift to the first hut.*"

Yes, it's true. The normal route up Europe's highest mountain isn't a particularly technical climb and after the ski lifts of the lower slopes peter out, 'Pisten Bully' piste bashers penetrate the middle slopes. In fact the Top Gear approach to mountain climbing doesn't stop there. If I tell you that a team of loonies even managed to manhandle a Landrover to the top of Elbrus in 1997 (even though it took them two attempts and forty three days) you'll probably think that climbing this mountain is for pussies (or for Jeremy Clarkson) - but you'd be very, very wrong. According to Wikipedia between fifteen and thirty people die climbing the mountain each year. That's more than the number of Everest fatalities. Sometimes ill-equipped, sometimes disorientated, sometimes falling off the mountain or into one of its crevasses, whatever the cause, make no mistake - climbing Elbrus is a serious undertaking. The mountain generates its own weather and has a reputation for changing its mind (further proof of its female characteristics perhaps?). Often producing ferocious gales, the mountain can quickly and easily plummet temperatures to minus twenty degrees centigrade and below. For that reason most climbers attempt Elbrus in the summer when summit temperatures on a good day are a more benign –5°C to –10°C.

Now in case you'd forgotten about that travel guardian angel of mine, I should point out that the week before arriving at Elbrus the weather was so atrocious that less than 1% of climbers (i.e. the ultra-hard-core-crazies) actually managed to make it to the summit. This piece of information was imparted to us by Maxim, our most wonderful Uzbek guide. We pondered it at Terskol in the sodding (stair rodding) rain. We pondered it as we ascended through claggy mist in two gondolas and a chairlift We pondered it as we shuffled slowly upwards through the cloud from the Garabashi botchki (barrel shaped) huts towards Diesel hut, at 4,060m (13,300ft). And we pondered it as we listened to the wind howling throughout our first night there.

Diesel hut oozes what an estate agent might describe as 'rustic charm'. The original three-story 'des res' Priut 11 refuge hut burnt down in 1998. Apparently an enthusiastic attempt to light a primus stove failed and an equally enthusiastic attempt to douse the flames with what turned out to be petrol rather than water contributed to the hut's total destruction. Work is currently underway to rebuild a refuge for climbers but in the meantime, if you're looking for a place with walls in which to sleep at over four thousand metres, it's going to have to be Diesel. The hut's rustic charm derives from the fact that it was designed to house a generator rather than the fifty or so climbers who now cosy up in various hardboard chambers. This makes for an unexpectedly comfortable if somewhat cramped existence, but when you're beginning to feel the effects of altitude, who's bothered? Aside from its basic nature, Diesel hut's other claim to fame is its outside privy. Straight from the Heath Robinson school of design, it juts out precipitously from the side of the hut, offering users a view unparalleled throughout the Caucasus – a slowly accumulating pile of mainly human detritus which I reckon has approximately twenty metres to grow before Dynarod has to be called out. Given the toilet cabin's flimsy construction and the gently swaying sensation whenever the wind blows (i.e. most of the time) I reckon that the shit pile's probably got another metre of growth - tops - before the privy collapses. After that the outlook will change from breath-holding to breathtaking, as the main Caucasus range with its panorama of pointy topped peaks and glistening glaciers suddenly reveals itself.

Sometimes the mountains wear a demure apron of cloud, sometimes they sport a jaunty cloud hat and on rare occasions they might shed their cloud cover completely, revealing all their naked glory. Visibility permitting, the Paramount Pictures landscape gets better and better as you get higher. Leaving behind the noise and detritus of Diesel hut you pass a giant boulder displaying a plethora of plaques to Russian climbers who have died attempting Elbrus and finally you break free from the infernal combustion engine. Above you the 5,620m (18,400ft) east summit of Elbrus beckons like a tall snow mane mount of happiness (actually it seemed more like a giant breast to me) and your footsteps head joyfully upwards. Well, perhaps not so much joyfully as breathlessly. It takes about three hours to reach the Pashtukhova rocks, the usual upper limit for snow mobiles. At this altitude - 4,640m (15,200ft) - you've passed the acclimatisation test for a summit attempt. Weather permitting and god willing the next day we would go for it!

That evening the group faced a dilemma. Should we take advantage of a snow mobile to give us a head start to the Pastukhova rocks, or should we be purists and climb under our own steam the extra three hours? We debated this question to and fro until it was pointed out by someone that as we had already used artificial means to reach Garabashi anyway, what difference did it make? When the votes were cast I cheerfully opted for the Top Gear approach to climbing and joined a majority vote for a snow-cat head start.

Fortified by haute altitude haute cuisine prepared by our star cook Sergei under the challenging conditions of Diesel hut's cramped kitchen, we turned in at 7pm to try and wrest some sleep from the next five hours. Let's just say that the expectation was a triumph of hope over experience. We arose at 1.45am, tired and trepidatious, fumbling and faffing and trying to remember all the bits of kit that would make or break our summit bid. In the confusion I managed to lose my special warm hat and had to make do with a Forestry Commission headpiece (my hat later emerged from under the bed: it clearly didn't fancy a twelve hour altitude stress test).

Sitting on the back seat of the open-air piste basher clattering up a thirty degree slope at three a.m. was a surreal experience. Some familiar and not a few unfamiliar constellations lit up the night sky with a million points of light. Watching the stars go by reminded me of Everest summit day fifteen months earlier and the extraordinary experience of staring down on stars. I could definitely get used to this effortless way of climbing mountains. But as the machine deposited us at 4,600m (15,000ft) we knew that the easy part was now over and the hard work was about to begin: a thousand metres of pure, undiluted slog towards the uttermost point of Europe.

There's a kind of out-of-body phenomenon about climbing at night. As the darkness swallows you up, all concepts of time and distance disappear. Your only point of reference is the light from your head torch. You gradually become lost in an otherworldly experience: just you, your thoughts, your heavy breathing and the inexorable upward shuffle of cramponed boots in soft snow. Above and below, other groups of climbers can be seen threading their way slowly up the mountainside like giant glow-worms. After some hours (or was it just a few minutes?) the faintest of orange lines appears in the east, preceding a dark purple crepuscular luminosity presaging the break of dawn. You realise with a shock that the stars have gradually disappeared and all the stuff you've been plodding through and up is actually white snow. Eventually the sun breaks the horizon and the magical panorama of a thousand snowy peaks emerges to the south and below. Sure, it was ass-freezing cold and every footprint filled with spindrift and we could now see the daunting upward challenge of the traverse - our next immediate challenge - but we were making progress! The all-important good weather was holding and my guardian angel was – I believe – smiling down and willing us to succeed.

The traverse is a one kilometre long slog round the shapely slope of Elbrus' eastern breast, ascending 300m (980ft) to the cleavage at 5,416m (17,800ft) separating Elbrus' Twin Peaks. Here are visible the vestiges of a hut which used to shelter climbers in trouble. Nowadays a helicopter can be summoned in extremis (and at a cost) to rescue stranded climbers, but it's a risky business: we were informed that the previous week a Russian MI-8 chopper carrying nine climbers crashed on Elbrus' West Ridge. Although everyone survived, the aircraft was a write-off (in 1991 eight people were killed in a similar accident). By now all twelve of us were suffering, the unlucky thirteenth member having made the wise and brave decision to turn back. That we had reached the saddle at all was a credit to the sheer bloody-minded determination of the team and the confidence-boosting encouragement of Maxim.

We paused at the saddle for a while, hearts hammering in the thin air, trying to unblock frozen water tubes and contemplating the next stage of the climb: a 200m (650ft) ascent of Elbrus' west breast, requiring ice axes and concentration. An unchecked slip would have resulted in injury on the rocks below – at best. After an hour of slow and steady climbing we reached a collection of boulders and at last started to turn southwards towards the summit. Maxim had told us that from this point the climb was less steep, even levelling out for a while before the summit nipple itself. Eight hours after setting out on 6th August 2008, when the west summit of Elbrus did eventually reveal itself to us, our pace picked up and we raced in slow motion towards the 5,642 (18,510ft) prize which is the top of Europe.

As we stood there at last, all the pain and agony of the last few hours was forgotten as we gazed down on the 360° panorama of peaks, glaciers and clouds, forgetting to check whether – as rumour has it – we could spy the Black Sea from the crow's nest of Europe. For a few minutes flags were unfurled, cameras clicked and memories captured as we relished mixed sensations: satisfaction, gratification and appreciation. Forget the Top Gear approach to climbing now – effort was the one true path to enlightenment: no pain, no gain. Each member of the team had different reasons for being there: each had different motivations. With summit temperatures only a few degrees below zero we wanted to remain forever. But Maxim wisely called time. It was a long way back down and we faced several gruelling hours of trudging through difficult snow conditions back to Diesel hut.

The Elbrus guardian angel was still kind to us as we descended slowly into oxygen-rich air. Summer afternoon conditions on the mountain can often deteriorate, turning the descent into an ordeal. Sometimes a more settled weather pattern heralds an uncomfortable descent – hot and dehydrating. But luckily for us a steady gentle wind cooled us down and helped our retreating footsteps.

With the Elbrus angel still in benign mood, our final day on the mountain dawned fine and clear. We descended the short distance from Diesel Hut to Garabashhi botchki admiring the stunning Caucasus mountain range which had so completely eluded us on the way up. But just before we reached the chairlift, Elbrus had one last surprise in store for us.

It must be something of a tradition for Russian girls to take their clothes off at altitude in the sunshine. Frankly these girls had it and they were definitely flaunting it. After all the discomfort and hardship and suffering of the last few days, here was a welcome sight for sore eyes: a definite sighting of 'angels on Elbrus'.

Two other members of the expedition comprised Pat Snowdon and John Vaughan, colleagues at the Forestry Commission.

Elbrus

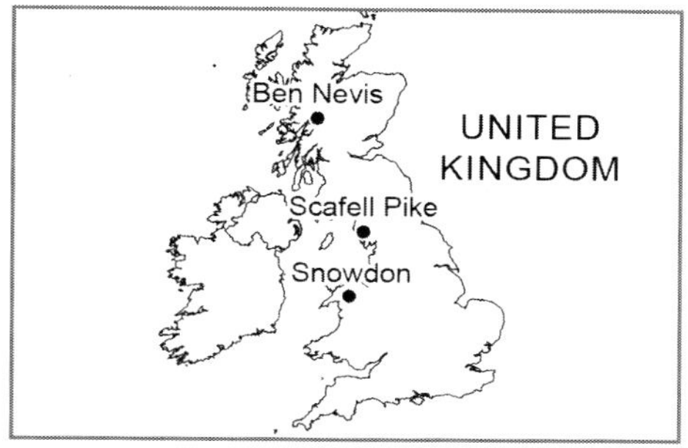

12

Cheeky Three Peakers (2009)

There's something a bit mad about wanting to climb The Big Three within the space of a day.

Climbing the highest mountains in Scotland, England and Wales in under twenty four hours is generally something you plan well in advance, but not in our case…

Question: Apart from a general lack of rational balance and mental sanity, what connects several hundred hill walkers assembling at Ben Nevis on a wet Friday summer's evening?

Answer: They're all about to tackle the Three Peaks in twenty four hours.

There's something a bit mad about wanting to climb Ben Nevis, Scafell Pike and Snowdon within the space of a day. For a start there's the miles of driving and associated sleep deprivation. Then there's the rain and midges and other hill walkers getting underfoot, not to mention the general hardship and effort required; when I recall our 'expedition' I feel a bit of a fraud. Apparently most folk spend weeks and months planning and training for 'The Big Three'. In our case the idea was a twinkle in the eye one week and reality the next, one of those rare instances that life throws at you where a madcap idea fell into place as if by magic.

I had recently come across an article in one of the outdoor magazines that went on about how awful and gnarly the whole Three Peaks experience was. The author wrote about how they only just made it, eventually reaching the top of Snowdon in just under twenty four hours (in my book that doesn't count though – you also have to come down) but it got me thinking, and talking, and as if by some mysterious force I began to encounter people who helped my germ of an idea to sprout. Well... sort of. Through a colleague at work, an eleventh hour possibility of joining an organised Three Peaks expedition eventually failed to materialise. Undeterred, I phoned Jane Watts, Librarian for Scottish Opera and Munro buddy, in case she might be interested.

She was. What's more she thought she might know of someone who could drive us. That was on the Friday. The following Monday she confirmed that Mick Green (a retired Met Office CID officer) was 'up for it'. With only a few days for the three of us to prepare for our 'international expedition to conquer the highest summits in three countries', it was suddenly a case of 'game on!'

That's why, at 5pm at the Glen Nevis Youth Hostel on a wet – no make that *stonkingly* wet – July evening, the three of us sat in Mick's car looking through the windscreen at hordes of hapless 'Three Peakers' trudging off into the middle distance like herds of wet sheep. Just as we prepared to 'scramble' Mick suggested, "*Why not leave it till six?*" As we weren't sufficiently mathematically minded to leave it until 5.28 or 5.47 for example, we quickly agreed (well, anything to avoid the rain) and continued watching the downpour from the comfort of the car.

As things turned out it was a good suggestion. The stair-rodding rain moved off to deluge another glen, leaving a more typical Fort William weather pattern: fine drizzle, limited visibility and midges. What we didn't realise until much later was that delaying the start was actually an advantage, timing-wise. When we reached the cloud-covered top of Ben Nevis after 'pushing the proverbial envelope' Jane and I did feel a little guilty about our muttered excuses to a group of summiteers who wanted their photos taken. "*Sorry, we're running late,*" I uttered over my shoulder (well, hell, this was after all a serious undertaking) as we turned on our heels and ran off down the runnable sections of path. Later, in preparation for a swift turnaround Jane texted Mick to say we were nearly back. "*What kept you?*" came back Mick's cheeky reply and in the end we made it to the car in a total of under four hours. A very good start! After quickly freshening up at the Youth Hostel we headed south in the gloaming towards our next goal - England's highest mountain.

Mick turned out to be a complete star. A skilful driver whose police training kept him the right side of legal, he had a limitless fund of entertaining stories and anecdotes, a great knack for getting us close to the starting and finishing points and a noble talent for just 'being there for us'. Most importantly he seemed to function quite normally with only the odd forty winks or so between long drives. All in all he took a proprietorial attitude towards his two charges, proudly announcing to anyone who would listen, that we were without doubt the fastest folk on the hills.

After our delayed start at Ben Nevis, Jane and I had not anticipated needing head torches. We had expected to reach Scafell Pike at between four and five am but in the event Mick dropped us at the head of Wast Water in complete darkness, at 3.30am precisely (luckily we could still just about cope with the maths). One of the surprises of this mountain malarkey was seeing so many other vehicles and people doing the same thing: instead of the four or five other groups that I had expected, a complete circus of three-peak-wannabes congregated at the foot of each climb. By virtue of simply being the highest, these mountains have attracted a lot of climbers and a lot of controversy. Is it right or wrong for their fragile environments to be subjected to the erosion of thousands of boot prints, not to mention the carbon footprints of countless cars and vans, the pressure on limited parking spaces and the trail litter? (Discuss). It was no surprise to see a digger halfway up Ben Nevis and large bags of trail ballast helicoptered onto the paths of both the Ben and Snowdon. Depressingly, one could see that previous efforts to stabilise paths on these steep slopes had met with subsequent washout and destruction. These delicate mountain environments are subject to harsh weather conditions. Add too many humans into the mix and you have a recipe for inevitable environmental damage.

The start of Scafell Pike was the trickiest from the navigation point of view. As we headed away from the car once more we observed random groups of torches bobbing here, there and everywhere, desperately searching for the right route. It called for some careful map reading to get us to the correct path (which we lost at one point) and away from odd pile of vomit (three peak pukers perhaps?). Yes, it was all very unpleasant at that dogwatch time of night. But we crept up and daylight crept in and just two hours later we found ourselves at the summit. Like Ben Nevis, Scafell Pike was wearing a blanket of low cloud and for the second time in our mission the anticipated view was cruelly denied. Confounding our quest for chronological simplicity by arriving back at the car three hours and five minutes later, we knew by now that – even allowing for contingencies – we should be able to complete Snowdon without time pressures.

There is however a sting in the tail for those rushing to complete the Three Peaks. It's a simple case of demand far outstripping supply, for the car park at Pen y Pass has only sufficient spaces for a few vehicles and on summer weekends the demand for parking greatly exceeds the available spaces. The nearest alternative is a long way down the road and also, inevitably, full to overflowing. In desperation, drivers resort to leaving their cars on the roadside and get back to find a parking ticket. We must have seen at least fifty such cars. I had been given dire warnings about the parking attendants at Pen y Pass by a former Three Peaker. "*They'll not even let you drop off there.*" But Mick's charm worked like a treat and Jane and I were allowed a few precious minutes to get ourselves kitted up for the final climb. What's more, when we eventually returned three hours and 45 minutes later, Mick had even managed to inveigle himself a parking space there.

Though not as wet as Glen Nevis, Snowdon managed to chuck precipitation at us for almost the whole climb. I had expected an easy ascent and descent of the famous Pyg track, but first of all there were several tricky washed-out sections and second of all there were far too many people slowing us down. I was quite shocked to see how many struggling, ill-equipped groups were there: people who should never have been on the mountain - and that was just on the way up. A score of Germans in trainers and jeans wearing plastic ponchos; lots of Indians in shell suits, turbans and trainers; kids without waterproofs or boots; seriously overweight Mums being supported on both sides by their children and finally some fit but mad youths carrying - of all things - bicycles. Although our 24-hour target was not in jeopardy, Jane and I both agreed that the ultimate frustration for a Three Peaker would be to get stuck behind these groups and thereby just miss the deadline.

So we forged on through the mist again (for the third time we were fated not to get a view) and eventually the bizarre chuff-chuff sound of a steam train reached our ears. For its last few metres the Pyg track runs alongside the famous Snowdon funicular railway that takes tourists - sitting down in comfort - to the top of Wales. Although we ourselves were also chuffed at reaching our third and final summit goal, it wasn't a particularly pleasant experience. The top was mobbed with people looking tired, cold and miserable and hoping to get a seat and a cuppa at Wales' highest café. No chance. The place was packed out. Jane and I decided to celebrate by getting out of the weather and into the café foyer to eat our packed lunch. Shortly afterwards a gleam entered my eye. When was I next going to get a chance to answer the call of nature in the highest public convenience in Wales? The temptation was too much to resist. And after all, we were well inside the 24-hour deadline…

One of the nice things about the Three Peaks challenge is recognising other climbers and giving each other mutual encouragement. On Scafell Pike we had recognised several climbers from Ben Nevis but as only a couple of familiar faces appeared on Snowdon I guessed we were ahead of the game. Back at the Pen y Pass car park Mick confirmed this when he said that most other groups were by now only just arriving. With the time standing at 2.30 we realised that most of them wouldn't make it up and down within the 24-hour deadline but we had done it with hours to spare and so we celebrated with a mutual hug and a group photo and a farewell wave to Mick's new best friend, the car park attendant. Then we headed down towards Llanberis for a cuppa, and the long journey back north.

Stopping off at Kirby Lonsdale for a joyful celebratory pub supper that evening, the triumphant threesome recalled the highs and lows of the last 24 hours and despite the befuddlement of a few pints, got to grips with the specifics of timing. With a total time taken of twenty and a half hours we all had reason to congratulate ourselves. But then a sudden thought hit me. If I hadn't decided to park myself on Snowdon's throne for a while and if we had shaved off the odd minute or two here and there, we could - without too much extra effort - have managed the Three Peaks in under *twenty* hours.

Now that would have been a result!

The other expedition members comprised Mick Green (driver extraordinaire) and Jane Watts who now runs Kiltyrie Farmhouse Bed & Breakfast near Loch Tay.

Expedition Statistics - Three peaks climbed on 3rd & 4th July 2009

Mountain	**Ben Nevis**	**Scafell Pike**	**Snowdon**	**Total**
Start time	6.00pm	3.30am	10.45am	
Summit arrival	8.30pm	5.30am	12.40pm[1]	
Return time	9.55pm	6.35am	2.30pm	
Total climbing time	3.55	3.05	3.20	10.20
Summit m/ft	1344m	978m	1085m	
Starting height m/ft	30m	65m	359m	
m/ft ascent	1314m/4308ft	913m/2993ft	726m/2380ft	2953m/9686ft[2]
Total distance km/mi	14.3km/8.9mi	4.2km/2.6mi	10.1km/6.3mi	28.6km/17.8mi

[1]Followed by 25 minutes before descending

[2]More metres of ascent than the height distance between Everest Advance Base camp and its summit.

A wet start at Glen Nevis

Summit of Ben Nevis

Summit of Snowdon

Summit of Scafell Pike

A wet finish at Pen y pass

Three Peaks - Ben Nevis, Scafell Pike, Snowdon

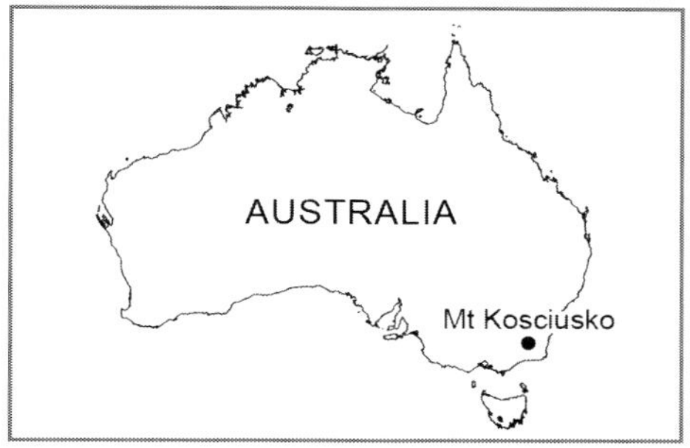

13

Aussie Kozzy – where the spirits dance (2010)

Easiest of the seven summits, Australia's highest mountain is a trek rather than an expedition, but no less enjoyable for that…

It all started in Edinburgh, before we had even set off for Australia. "*It's not pronounced Kos-i-us-co, it's Kosh-zhis-kŏ: three syllables, not four*". Micha's eyes lit up as she continued, "*Koshisko was from Poland – he was an ancestor of mine!*" This unlikely revelation came from the mother of the family that had agreed to take teenager James into their bosom for the three weeks that Sarah and I had booked 'down under'. When we explained to Micha the main reason for our trip - to climb Mt Kosciuszko, the highest mountain in Australia - she enlightened us about her ancestor of the same name: a Polish freedom fighter who lived from 1746 to 1817, fought in the American Revolutionary war, led Poland's last struggle for independence against Russia, and eventually became a citizen of the United States.

The peak was christened in 1840 by a Polish-Australian explorer called Paul Strzelecki. He named it Kosciusko because it reminded him of the eponymous Mound in Krakow – an artificial hill thirty four metres tall, constructed to commemorate the Polish national hero. Whilst exploring this corner of Australia, Strzelecki wrote: "*The particular configuration of this eminence struck me so forcibly by the similarity it bears to the tumulus elevated in Krakow over the tomb of the patriot Kosciusko that, although in a foreign country, in foreign ground, but amongst a free people who appreciate freedom and its votaries, I could not refrain from giving it the name of Mount Kosciusko.*"

Thus this corner of a foreign field is forever associated with Poland, a little known fact that explains why so many Polish visitors are attracted to the area today.

In reality Australia's highest mountain turned out to be much less shapely that its Krakow counterpart and I wonder whether Strzelecki might not have confused it with the continent's second highest peak - Mount Townsend - when he wrote about... "*A pinnacle, rocky and naked, predominant over several others*". Before closing this history lesson, I should add a footnote on the mountain's spelling. Proponents of political correctness have campaigned to add a 'z' to the name, asserting that Kosciuszko is a more accurate reflection of the Polish spelling. However, to most Aussies none of this pedantry matters a jot: to them, Australia's highest mountain is simply and affectionately nicknamed 'Kozzy'!

Exponents of seven summiteering differ in their view as to what constitutes the seventh continent. To some, it's Oceania, making the highest peak 'Carstenz Pyramid' (Puncak Jaya) in Papua New Guinea: at 4,884 metres (16,000ft) over twice the height of Kosciusko. To others it's Australia, which makes Kozzy the baby of the seven by a long way, at only 2,228m (7,300ft), but this relativity is only an accident of geology and time. Unlike brash new landscapes such as the Himalayas, Andes and New Zealand Alps, where some mountains are gradually increasing in height through colossal tectonic forces, the Australian Alps have been steadily eroded by millions of years of ice, wind and rain to become mere shadows of their former self. This, then, is a truly ancient landscape, a timeless 'dreamtime' landscape which - like so many other high places in the world - seems more real than reality itself.

This means that climbing Kosciuszko is a trek rather than an expedition: you can complete it comfortably in a shortish day, although in an effort to appear a bit more gnarly some seven summiteers 'sex up' their experience by doing it when the Snowy Mountains are actually snowy, adding another photo to their collection of white summits. As for Sarah and me, we were quite content to do the trek in February - the tail end of summer in the southern hemisphere and not a vestige of snow in sight.

Kosciuszko mountain retreat lies just within the eponymous National Park in New South Wales. This place consists of seven thousand square kilometres of rugged mountains and fragile alpine wilderness. Having arrived at the campground late and in the dark, we were totally unprepared for the spectacle that greeted us the next morning: several wild kangaroos happily hopping about beneath the gum trees. There was absolutely no doubt about which continent we were on now.

Thoughts of breakfast were pushed aside in a frenzied photofest. Later - when hunger eventually overtook us - the Joeys seemed perfectly content to queue up for a campervan breakfast which eventually ended in an undignified tussle for the cornflakes (the Kangaroos won). Somehow our stereotypical view of large, timid creatures in the outback had to adjust to accommodate their smaller, mountain-dwelling relatives, busily bouncing about the Great Dividing Range and cheekily consuming their continental breakfast with a couple of crazy Pommies.

The short drive by campervan to the Kosciusko trailhead passes through Perisher, a purpose-built ski village within the largest snow resort in the southern hemisphere (it's difficult not to think of it as Perishing in winter – which it probably is). Like all purpose-built ski villages that are vibrant and pulsating during the season, Perisher appeared rather incongruous and forlorn in the Australian summer sunshine, but it did produce two startlingly unexpected revelations for us.

The first was the best BLT sandwich in the Universe. The second – and you're not going to believe this - was an underground railway station. No, I'm not joking: there's an eight kilometre train track tunnelled into the mountains here (maximum incline 12.5%, maximum depth 550m) to enable skiers to reach otherwise inaccessible slopes. I'm not talking about a funicular railway to get you up to the high pistes. No, this is effectively an underground system in the middle of a National Park wilderness in the flattest and smallest of the earth's seven continents. In one's relentless quest for the seven summits, it doesn't get much stranger than that …

The tarmac road runs out at Charlotte (or Charlotte's) Pass (1,837m/6,000ft). Charlotte Adams was the first European woman to climb Mount Kosciuszko, back in 1881. Although there is no recorded account of the very first European ascent, stockmen undoubtedly roamed the area from the 1830s onwards in search of summer pastures and for thousands of years before that it is certain that Aboriginal peoples knew this mountain range.

Indeed according to Aboriginal oral tradition, Kosciusko has a special spiritual significance. For thousands of years Aborigines from all directions visited these mountains to participate in ceremonies, learn from their ancestors' stories and feast on the bogong moths which congregate here in summer. However, for reasons of spiritual deference, these seasonal guests rarely went to the highest tops, closest to the stars, where their ancestral spirits are believed to dance.

From Charlotte's Pass it's an easy five mile walk up to the top of Australia, for this was once a driveable dirt road. There are interpretive panels showing old cars toiling up to Rawson's Pass, not far from the summit, but because of overuse, vehicles were banned in 1976, since when the road has been a walking track. That explains why it's such a pleasure to hike here: the skilful Aussie engineers constructed an easy gradient that threads gently up through the snow gum tree line, winding around the contours and becoming part of the landscape rather than fighting it.

After leaving the last of the stunted snow gums behind, you enter the alpine zone. As you might expect, these alpine areas are rare indeed in Australia: within the Kosciusko National Park there are only two hundred and fifty square kilometres (ninety six square miles) of the stuff (a mere four percent of the Park area) and it drops to around one percent around Mt Kosciusko itself. This ecosystem is a windswept patchwork quilt of alpine heaths, herb fields, bogs and fens which must have been tiresome indeed to traverse before 1906 when the road was constructed. Our route was a gentle gravel surface with plenty of hidden culverts to keep the surface dry and numerous weather-beaten snow poles to show the route in winter.

In fact our biggest concern during the three hour ascent was not the ground conditions but the notorious Australian sunshine: without proper protection you can quickly fry in these ozone-challenged conditions. But the mountain gods were smiling on us that day and we were lucky in many respects. For a week beforehand there had been unseasonably heavy rain that had thwarted all but the most committed of climbers, whereas our summit day was characterised by light clouds, sunshine and good visibility.

Two thirds of the way up sits the first of two structures on the route - Seaman's Hut - built by the New South Wales tourist bureau in 1929 following a mountaineering tragedy. This survival shelter is a memorial to Laurie Seaman who, along with another climbing companion, died whilst descending Kosciusko on 13th August 1928. Lest one underestimate the power of this or indeed any other mountain, Seaman's Hut contains another memorial commemorating the lives of four young snowboarders who died of exposure near here on 7th August 1999.

At Rawson's Pass (2,100m/6,900ft) our track was joined by another, shorter route to the summit: a four mile mesh walkway accessed by a chairlift ride from the ski resort of Thredbo. This route has proved so popular by the estimated 100,000 or so people who now visit the mountain each summer that it required the construction of Australia's highest public conveniences in 2007 (and yes, we did, thanks). After the peace and quiet of our gentle ascent from Charlotte's Pass we were now painfully aware of chattering young Japanese tourists and older intrepid Australian trekkers. The surprise to us was a seeming lack of younger Australian hikers. '*Do young Aussies not get out into the mountains,*' we wondered? '*Perhaps they were off on less popular routes?*'

As the last hundred metres of path circled around towards the top of the continent it revealed views of the Great Dividing Range: long ridges, deep valleys and distant blue horizons. Then the vista became a whole three hundred and sixty degree panorama as the 2,228 metre (7,310 ft) summit cairn of Kosciusco came into view.

We waited patiently for the chattering groups of tourists to depart this hallowed ground so sacred to the Aboriginal people - and now sacred to me as the sixth and penultimate summit of my global adventure. Finally, it happened. The cameras stopped clicking, the throng dispersed and peace broke out on top of Mt Kosciusco. We had reached the highest point in Australia, closest to the stars, where the ancestral spirits of the Aboriginal people danced. I resisted the temptation to dance and instead reflected, communing for a while with the spirits of the Snowy Mountains…

In David Horton's Encyclopedia of Aboriginal Australia (1994) there is a wonderful quote: *People come and go, but the Land, and stories about the Land, stay. This is a wisdom that takes lifetimes of listening, observing and experiencing.... There is a deep understanding of human nature and the environment... sites hold 'feelings' which can not be described in physical terms...*

In the summit silence it was almost possible to capture the hint of an echo of those feelings. Perhaps one day we too could come to experience a deeper dreamtime understanding.

Finally, the time to descend approached. The last word belongs to some Aboriginal advice to be found on a plaque at Rawson's Pass: "*Everything should be respected – especially the big rocks and the high mountain tops. The spirits of our old people (the early travellers) who came here still live on in them. Please go quietly, please go respectfully*".

Not a bad creed for all those who love the mountains.

Sarah Graham danced on Kozzy with the Aboriginal ancestral spirits.

Kosciusko

Rwenzori

14

Limpet the lamb – a cautionary tale for all Munro baggers (2010)

Beware adhesive small animals – especially if they're in the shape of a little lamb with attitude…

I never wanted to be a Mum. One minute I was striding out on my own across the Scottish wilderness and the next minute a small white creature bolted towards me and attached itself - limpet like - about my person, or more accurately my legs. In fact it tripped me up in full stride.

As I collapsed in a heap on the ground I was vaguely conscious of a feeble "*baa*" coming from beneath me. '*That's a lamb,*' I thought to myself as I hit the heather. Simultaneously my brain: a) told me not to be so stupid - lambs don't trip up humans; and b) figured that I had tripped over a quartz rock instead. Picking myself up from the heather I glanced down. '*That's a lamb*,' my brain told me again as I beheld a small white ungulate with a small black face looking up endearingly.

"*Go away*," I ordered crossly, brushing away heather stalks from my jacket.

"*Baa*".

This encounter wasn't in my hill walking plans. Clearly the thing was disoriented and confused. In a moment of stupidity it had latched on to me thinking I was its Mum. How bizarre. Oh well, it would soon enough realise the error of its ways.

"*Baaa*".

I looked around for a ewe. She would surely be close by: the big one looking all worried and maternal.

Nothing. Not a mutton sausage to be seen. Only the lively lamb chop nudging at my feet in a display of youthful affection.

"*Bugger off home!*" I commanded in a stern and threatening tone of voice.

"*Baaaa*".

"*OK*," I said to myself, "*not a problem. I'll simply run off and leave it to be discovered by its real mum in the near future.*" So without a backward glance I legged it as fast as I could, happy at having solved this minor irritation; but less than a minute later a horribly familiar little nudging sensation could be felt at the back of my legs. And there it was again, the blasted critter. This was beginning to get seriously annoying…

Now just ahead of me was the Abhainn Ghlas: more of a raging torrent than a trickle despite recent dry weather. "*Aha!*" I said to myself. "*That's the answer. No way is that little limpet going to cross that big obstacle.*" So, jumping from rock to precarious rock as the river surged all around, I eventually hauled myself up the steep soft bank beyond and onto terra firma. I looked back smugly. No lamb on my side of the river. Result! But wait a minute… where was the little bleater? Not - as I expected - standing pathetically on the other side and howling, or whatever it was that lambs do. So where was it then?

I returned to the river and there, nestled into the bank, was the bedraggled cruciform shape of lambkin, its front legs splayed pathetically into the soil and its back legs still in the water, unable to move either up or down. I couldn't imagine how on earth it had got across the torrent. Great! Now I had a half-dead creature on my hands, baahooing plaintively. Things were going from bad to worse…

Still listening in vain for the maternal bleating of a distressed ewe, I picked up this pathetic ball of wet fur and tried to dry it as best as I could. But despite its near-death experience, it quickly regained its composure and once again started trotting close behind me up the track. Although I was relieved that it seemed none the worse for wear I was still annoyed by its leech-like tendencies. There was another Munro to be climbed and time was fast slipping away. This was beginning to resemble one of those true life stories where the experienced Everest mountaineer has to abandon his summit bid after encountering another climber in trouble… except that this was a lamb (even if it was starting to seem almost human by now) and not a climber. Mind you the little blighter had stamina, I'll say that for him.

Eventually an opportunity presented itself in the confusing terrain and I seized my chance to give it the slip amongst a baffling series of undulations. I ran like hell and hid behind a bluff. At last, a sheep-free zone! Sneaking a peek from behind the vegetation I saw Limpet - for this was what I had mentally christened him by now - looking pathetically this way and that, before sitting down and appearing just as miserable as only a little lambkin could. Half guilty but wholly relieved, I carefully clocked its whereabouts and continued on my way towards the next mountain. '*If it's still there by the time I return*,' I thought to myself, '*I may have to do something about it,'* and happily put the matter out of my mind for the next two hours or so.

As I descended Beinn Mhanach, my thoughts turned to what the future might bring. *'If Limpet's still there when I return I can't just leave him. He's only two or three days old: the buzzards will surely get him. I'll have to rescue him from certain death.'*

That was my angel side talking.

But my devil side pointed out that it would still be a ten kilometre hike across rough trackless terrain up and over a pass 770m (2,500ft) high – and that was just back to where I had left my bike at the foot of Creag Mhor. From there it would be another three quarters of an hour's cycle ride to where I had parked the car. And by now it was five o'clock in the evening.

The moment of truth approached as I arrived at the place where I had abandoned Limpet. Would a mad white furry orphan still be there – and would he still recognise his giant of a mother again?

Dammit – he did!

In a repetition of our first encounter he rushed towards me exuding affection from every fibre of his fluffy white fleece. Mum had returned and all was right with the world!

As I picked up little Limpet to give him a cuddle, my devil side knew when he was beaten. "*Please yourself,*" he snarled, disappearing over my shoulder, "*on your head be it*".

So the epic homeward adventure began. It started well enough as I prepared a lamb-sized comfort zone for Limpet in my rucksack. "*It's OK, little one,*" I remarked, "*Your bed is a fleece, but it's acrylic, so no worries.*"

"*Baaa.*" He clearly understood. We were definitely on the same wavelength now and the bond between us was growing ever stronger. Feeling smug and self-righteous I started humming 'Little lamb who made thee' as I strode over the heather towards home, mentally congratulating myself on having solved the problem so brilliantly.

But it's true what they say: you should never work with children and animals. And you should definitely never work with childish animals. Although Limpet and I started our journey well (I could just see his little head peeking out of the rucksack flap, swaying from side to side) after a few minutes there was an uncommon commotion followed by a flying lamb and a brief "*Ba-*" as he hit the ground.

"*Bother!*" More delay. Well maybe it would knock sense into his numb lambskull.

It didn't. After a couple more instances of ungulate aerobatics I decided that it was high time to put my hoof down and make a stand. He could bloody well walk now. "*Let's see how you like that, eh?*" I snarled at him while he snuggled himself devotedly around my legs once more.

Clearly unfazed by my hostility, little Limpet continued to bounce along behind his mum. My cunning plan to tire him out before attempting to carry him again took far longer than I anticipated. It was only after a full mile of ascent and multiple burn crossings that he started to drop behind a little and bleat pathetically, his small white flanks heaving with the exertion of it all. Clearly little Limpet was a fighter. I liked that. In a change of heart - and tactic - I picked him up and gently tucked him into the front of my fleece. With his handsome black head poking out, we continued our way homewards. And although we now resembled kangaroo and joey more than ewe and lamb, at least Limpet didn't struggle like before.

I could say much about the magic of that still spring evening: the setting sun casting shadows on the corries and flanks of the hills; the red deer striking romantic Landseer poses; the ravens croaking evocatively and a complete absence of any other human beings. Little Limpet and I made a great team as the distance gradually shrank and the shadows gradually lengthened. And as we forged through the miles towards civilisation and safety, strains of Taverner gave way to The Proclaimers "*And I would walk five hundred miles and I would walk five hundred more*"; and "*We're on our way from loneliness to happiness today (u-huh, u-huh, u-huh, u-huh)*".

After reaching my bike at eight o'clock the happiness factor did indeed increase. Limpet was now zipped up safe and snug inside my fleecy pouch, paying no heed to the ups, downs, bangs and bumps of the rough Landrover track, until, just as darkness fell, we reached the security of the car. By now a seasoned traveller, Limpet was content to stay in the passenger floor well gently swaying to the road's twists and turns, and taking to his third means of transport that evening like, well, like a duck to water.

The next problem was - where to go next? Now call me heartless, but taking a lamb to live in an Edinburgh garden seemed a tad unfair on the neighbours, not to mention Jasper the Irish Setter. His proclivity towards sheep had already earned him a sheepish reputation. Limpet and Jasper? No, I just couldn't see it, somehow.

Happily, a solution to this problem appeared half an hour later in the shape of Kiltyrie Farmhouse Bed & Breakfast and the form of Jane, its owner.

"*Hi Jane! Long time no see. I'm bringing a friend to stay tonight if that's OK*".

It wasn't really. I mean who would drop everything to be a foster carer for a four legged un-house-trained peeing machine, I ask you?

Jane did. Without demur. That's the kind of person she is.

And at that, a burden lifted from me, both physically and metaphorically: I was sheep-free at last!

But when it came to bidding little limpet farewell I found it much harder than I'd expected. This wretched creature that had tripped me up, nearly thwarted my Munro plans and taken a herculean effort to rescue, had strangely grown on me.
Although I would never admit it, I'd come to love little Limpet.

There's a happy ending to this story. Jane phoned the next day to tell me that a local farmer's ewe - who had lost her lamb that morning - had happily adopted Limpet as her own.

What a relief: I'd never have made a good Mum anyway!

Baaa!

The other member of this expedition was a little white lamb called Limpet.

Sgurr nan Gillean and Am Bastier by moonlight

The Skye Ridge

The In Pin's north face

15

Grandmother's footsteps - a Saga Tours traverse of the Skye Ridge (2014)

You don't have to be a grandmother to climb the Cullin Ridge - but it helps...

Some dream demons decided to wake me up at around midnight and remind me of my age. "*Was I becoming too old for this malarkey?*" I wondered as I emerged from the warm security of my bivvy[1] bag , fumbled for my glasses and took in the surrounding scenery. In an instant all those doubts disappeared and I knew that this was where I was born to be...

Below our mountain eyrie and on the western horizon lingered the sunset silhouettes of Rhum, Eigg and Canna. Below and to the east, orange scintillas pinpointed Mallaig's distant street lights. Above our small stone shelter high up on a bealach[2] shone our long-cherished goal, the jagged peaks of the Cuillin Ridge, washed by the full moon's pale radiance. "It doesn't get much better than this," I realised as I slowly took it all in.

The Skye Ridge – or Cuillin Ridge – is by popular acclaim 'the most spectacular mountain scenery in the British Isles'. Iconic by anyone's standards, this is the only UK massif to approach the raw splendour of the Alps or the Rockies. Here lie no fewer than eighteen individual tops, fourteen over 3,000ft (914m) and eleven classed as Munros[3], all jostling within a seven mile crescent of volcanic rock nestled in south west Skye. Playground to climbers for over a hundred and fifty years, the Black Cuillins (not to be confused with their smaller cousins the Red Cuillins) have exerted a literally magnetic pull for generations of wannabe 'rock stars', hardcore climbers and Munro baggers. For the latter, McNeish[4] reminds us that the Cuillin Ridge represents the 'dark side': severe exposure, knife-edged ridges, steep scrambles and, of course, the infamous

[1]Bivouac bag.
[2]A narrow mountain pass.
[3]Munros are 3,000ft (914.4m) or higher. There are 282 Munros and 509 Munro tops.
[4]http://en.wikipedia.org/wiki/Cameron_McNeish

'In Pin' – the most technically difficult of all two hundred and eighty two Munros (of which more anon). Although the record for traversing the ridge is a bonkers three hours, most normal people take two days to do it. For although you might be forgiven for thinking that this sharp ridge is a kind of A to B experience with little room for getting lost, in fact the opposite is true: it's a veritable maze of confusing tracks, blind alleys and dodgy drop-offs. So not wishing to become 'dead ends' ourselves, Munro buddy Jane and I decided that hiring a good guide would be the first essential step along the way.

From the moment that Mike Pescod[5] arrived in his white 'Abacus Guides' van, he instilled confidence in his two tender charges. Veteran of a score of Cuillin traverses, wayfinder, diviner of hidden water and general comforter, Mike started the ball rolling by examining our rucksacks. Not having had time to pack carefully I had filled my monster seventy litre pack with spare trousers, gaiters, kitchen sinks and other paraphernalia while Jane on the other hand had packed Alpine style with only the bare essentials. Mike took one look at my rucksack and immediately started to discard a range of non-essential items. I sheepishly mumbled something about being 'in training' and sneaked in an inner sleeping bag when his back was turned. Having sorted out our kit, some water and food sufficient for a two day expedition (mainly tasty tiffin) we decided to get an early night. At least that was the plan…

Starting point for many Cuillin adventures is Sligachan – or 'Slig' as it's affectionately known by climbers. Slig is the base for exploring the northern Cuillins: Sgurr nan Gillean, Am Bastier and Bruach na Frithe. Now before I go much further (and call me a Sassenach philistine if you like) to this day I find pronouncing most Gaelic words a bit like a bad case of catarrh (and as far as remembering them? well forget it - so to speak). So, for the benefit of other Gaelic dyslexics out there I will offer English translations to aid mental retention as we proceed. So that would be *Peak of the Young Men*, (meaning obscure although I have my suspicions) and *Slope of the Deer Forest.*

Mike decided to initiate his Saga tour supplicants by a testing ascent of **Sgurr nan Gillean** and **Am Bastier.** Not for us the comforts of the 'tourist route', oh no. We were baptised into a full-on climb of Pinnacle Ridge, involving a couple of abseils and some 'airy' scrambles - including Knight's Peak lying between Sgurr nan Gillean and Am Bastier. This was named after W. Knight, who, with a guide, made its first recorded ascent in 1873. For years Knight's Peak was recorded as a Munro Top[6] at 3,002 feet but in 2013 a GPS resurvey found it to be six and a half inches shorter

[5]http://www.abacusmountaineering.com/currentconditions.html twitter.com/mikepescod
[6]A Munro Top is a satellite peak of a Munro being over 3,000ft but without significant height drop between the two peaks.

and it was unceremoniously demoted. But these mathematical niceties did not distract us from some demanding rock concentration and after acquitting ourselves in the climbing department we were deemed worthy to start the full ridge the next day. The forecast was encouraging and we were fit. "*So that's all good,*" said Mike as he left us for the evening.

At the other end of the ridge from Sligachan lies Glenbrittle Youth Hostel. Whilst Slig bunkhouse is situated conveniently close to its eponymous hotel (handy for celebratory jollifications) Glenbrittle YH is much quieter, a wee gem of a place recently refurbished and furnished in a homage to its 1939 origins. Black and white photographs on the dining room walls showed happy, chatty hostellers, while yesteryear memorabilia included a canvas and steel rucksack complete with jaunty leather straps – clearly the height of 'climber chic' in its day. I examined this bit of history more closely and then did a double take, suddenly feeling like a dinosaur. OK, it was true that I qualified for Saga holidays but didn't I possess just such a rucksack in my boy-scouting days? I decided to 'keep shtum'.

You get to meet some great people at hostels. The nickname 'Garrulous Tony' might seem to contradict this statement but he turned out to be a wonderfully entertaining hosteller. I'm guessing that there aren't too many other ex-Paratroop postmen out there with a fear of heights who have not only climbed all the Cuillins but recited a carefully selected poem at the top of each one. Then there was 'Glamorous Chloe' with bare feet and painted toenails, who regaled us with her insouciant approach to traversing Britain's most demanding ridge: "*So me and three other medic friends are going to climb it in one long day without overnighting,*" she announced with chutzpah. Knowing that the traverse comprises over 4,000m (13,000ft) of ascent and descent and usually takes around twenty hours in ideal weather conditions (assuming you don't get lost that is) I resisted the temptation to suggest that they take some shelter with them. "*And so we're getting up at 3am to get an early start,*" she added. I prayed to the hill gods that her party wouldn't be in the room next door.

They were…

Still, the sun was shining and the birds were singing when 'Tour Saga' set off from the idyllic campsite at Glenbrittle some four hours later. The only fly in my ointment (apart from a very interrupted night's sleep) was the weight of my backpack. Never had tiffin seemed so heavy. Huffing and puffing behind Mike and Jane I passed a rock that looked for all the world like Postman Pat's van. "*Was I hallucinating already?*" I wondered. "*Would a black and white cat suddenly appear too?*" But after a while we reached the small but perfectly formed loch Coir' a' Grunnda nestled in the mountains' southern fold. This would become a frequent landmark over the next few hours as we climbed up the Cuillin's southernmost peaks - **Sgurr nan Eag** (appropriately translated as *Rocky Peak of the Notch*) and **Sgurr Dubh Mor** (*Big Black Peak*). En route Mike allowed us to leave our packs in order to make summit sorties. I felt like Christian in Pilgrim's Progress when released from his heavy load (although I bet Christian wasn't advised to put his rucksack face down to avoid the canny ravens unzipping them and feasting on tiffin. But that's where you can't beat a little local knowledge from a guide who knows. No way was a ravenous raven gonna peck that tasty tiffin...)

The Black Cuillin of Skye is the spiritual home of scrambling. The term 'scrambling' means different things to different people but in essence it describes the cross-over from hill-walking to technical climbing: the boundary at which hill-walkers become mountaineers. You often need to use your hands, but good balance and footwork are also very important. And whilst you're usually prepared for the physical demands of the experience, nobody tells you about the exhausting mental effort required. Add into this mix the Cuillin ridge's exposure or 'airiness', with lots of opportunities for falling off, and you have an altogether challenging experience (I believe the technical term given for this powerful combo is 'ballsy', although I may be wrong). Those climbers who traverse the whole ridge in one go will doubtless have words of advice to others but I have only two suggestions: choose fine weather (the views are too good to squander on the altar of Munro bagging) and choose a reliable guide. It saves much time (on abortive route finding) and money (on repeated attempts).

Next up on our bagging list was **Sgurr Alasdair**, at 992m (3,255ft) the highest island mountain in Britain and allegedly named for Alexander Nicolson - a gaelic scholar and lawyer who made the first recorded ascent in 1873. One of the many advantages of a ridge traverse is that you get to bypass tiresome stuff, like the 'Great Stone Chute' for instance – a long and steep scree field leading up from Coire Lagan. Grateful to be above the chaotic stonefield we looked down on to some toiling figures below and then scrambled up to admire the fabulous views from Sgurr Alasdair's narrow summit perch. After this was **Sgurr Mhic Choinnich** (*Mackenzie's Peak*, named after the Victorian local mountain guide John MacKenzie, who made several first ascents in the Cuillin). This climb was described in the guidebooks as a 'serious scramble' and so it turned out to be, with some pretty exposed summit slabs. At one stage we looked across to a very steep rock face, wondering how we were going to get round it. Mike pointed out a groove etched into the cliff side. "*That's Collie's ledge,*" he said. It became apparent that our route comprised this so-called promenade. To us it looked like a via ferrata[7] only without the ferrata, but the reality was actually very different - a unique kind of Lord of the Rings' secret passageway which - once you've experienced it - is one of the secret charms of this extraordinary ridge: God's staircase in the snakes and ladders board game that characterises the Cuillins. The summit of Mhic Choinnich is a tiny eyrie marked with a weather-worn marble memorial in loving memory of Lewis Macdonald, a local climber. Trying to cast away morbid thoughts of new memorials, we knew that Skye Ridge's most notorious landmark - the Inaccessible Pinnacle - would be next…

For many centuries these forbidding west coast peaks were regarded as unclimbable. Being a forester it made me ridiculously happy to learn that amongst the first people to scramble up here was a local forester called Duncan MacIntyre. I think he would have approved of my 'going corporate' and wearing my trusty Forestry Commission waterproof, even if Mike pointed out that it was in fact quite bulky and heavy. In 1836, Professor James Forbes - an eminent scientist whose exploits in the Alps earned him the title 'Father of British Mountaineering' - hired MacIntyre as guide. Forbes noted the great steepness of the mountains and the roughness of the gabbro rock. He wrote, "*I have never seen a rock so adapted for clambering*". The Cuillin rock's roughness is due to its volcanic origins: gabbro, dolerite and basalt are actually all chemically identical but the roughness of gabbro is due to the presence of large crystals, formed by slower cooling of the molten rock. By contrast, basalt weathers down to a smooth surface and is slippery when wet. Gabbro was our friend: Jane and I christened it 'Grippy Gabbro' whilst Mike called it 'Happy Rock'. Having advised me on day one to eschew my trusty Black Diamond leather gloves, he instead lent me a pair of leather gardening gloves (no, really). But this turned out to be another top tip from a top guide. Better to wear out a cheap pair of leather gloves than ruin an expensive pair of climbing gloves.

Eventually the dreaded 'In Pin' crept up on us. It's a narrow fin of rock sticking up from the south side of **Sgurr Dearg** (*Red Peak*) and overtopping it by eight metres. As the only summit in the British Isles which has to be reached by rock climbing, it's the nemesis of many hillwalkers' ambitions to climb all two hundred and eighty two Munros. First climbed by Charles and Lawrence Pilkington in 1880, it was never actually climbed by Sir Hugh Munro himself. Unlike much of the Cuillin, the pinnacle is unhappy basalt and therefore slippery when wet. Happily for us we had ideal conditions, with unbroken views in every possible direction (including downwards). Jane started slowly up the moderate east face and then faltered. "*You ok?*" I asked. "*Remember, I'm a grandmother,*" she said plaintively: "*I have to take grandmother's footsteps.*"

[7] A via ferrata ('iron road') is a protected climbing route found e.g. in the Alps, comprising a steel cable periodically fixed to the rock, to which climbers secure themselves. There may be other climbing aids, e.g. iron rungs, pegs, carved steps, ladders and bridges. Thus via ferrata allow otherwise dangerous routes to be undertaken without the risks associated with unprotected scrambling and climbing or the need for climbing equipment.

Whereupon I suggested that she didn't 'look behind her' (or below her, come to that). After the first pitch she encountered two rock climbers popping up from their ascent of the south face. "*What do I do now?*" she entreated. "*Keep calm and carry on scrambling*," came their amused rejoinder. Later on Jane said that she had been far too busy concentrating on her tunnel vision to 'mind the gap'.

Hard-core climbers like to stand on the very top of the In Pin but I was content merely to anoint it with my hand, admiring the panoramic view for a while before abseiling the twenty metres or so to the ground. Job done. But just then who should form a surprise greeting party at this point but none other than Chloe and the doctors, off-schedule but still forging ahead with aplomb.

The only remaining Munro in our sights that day was the fine pointed summit of **Sgurr na Banachdich** (*Smallpox Peak* – now that's easy to remember!) a meeting point of three great scrambling ridges, one of the easiest Cuillin Munros and the exact mid-point of the Cuillin Ridge. With some relief we learned that this would be the sixth and final Munro of the day. Although this volcanic ridge is also noted for an almost complete absence of vegetation from its higher slopes some tiny alpines do manage to cling to crevices in the rocks and some, like alpine rock-cress, aren't found anywhere else in the UK. I became 'treemendously' happy when Mike introduced us to a friend of his – a Sitka spruce nestling into some rocks at about 900 metres (2,900ft) in altitude. "Could this hold the record for the highest Sitka in Scotland" I wondered? Only awaiting us now was a wee scramble to the bealach[8] below Sgurr a Greadaidh. Pronounced Greta, I naively imagined it to be named after Garbo, but in truth the translation is *Peak of Torment:* quite why I have no idea. Feeling well contented we made a trio of happy campers that evening feasting on tikka, tea and tasty tiffin and watching the sun slowly descend into the western sea.

Next morning started off well but it's true what they say about a red sky in the morning and it all went a bit 'Pete Tong' by lunchtime. First up on day two was *Sgurr a'Ghreadaidh,* which boasts two summits separated by the narrowest arete[9] in the British Isles. John Mackenzie was aged just fourteen when he climbed it (not for him the Saga Tours approach then). In fact Mackenzie is considered the first British mountain guide and arguably the most prolific of the Cuillin mountaineering pioneers.

---

[8]Mountain pass.

[9]A thin, almost knife-like, ridge of rock.

Memories of the last Munro that day became rather blurred as the rain increased from a steady downpour into a veritable deluge. Two awkward steps (that I later recalled as being like rock crevasses) required a lot of 'bottle' to cross. Lucky for us, Mike had a cunning work-around for the second step (unhappy basalt and very slippery). **Sgurr a'Mhadaidh** (*Peak of the Red Fox*) was the next top. Of its four summits, the highest is the only one that does not necessitate technical climbing. More rejoicing. We were not in the mood for rock climbing really. In fact we were not in the mood for anything much but completing our expedition. So when Mike asked us whether we wanted to carry on up Naismith's route (a serious rock climb) and repeat Sgurr nan Gillean and Am Bastier again, before you could say 'catarrh' we declined and instead headed up **Bruach na Frithe** famed for being one of the best viewpoints in the Cuillin. (Apparently. We couldn't see much more than the Ordnance Survey column on top). After that it was a case of skirting above the snow slopes to the north of Am Bastier towards the now-familiar track leading to Slig – and civilisation…

All in all we were pretty pleased really, having pretty well completed the traverse in two days. The first recorded traverse of the Cuillins in less than twenty four hours was in 1911 by Messrs Shadbolt and McLaren. The unbelievable speed record for the full traverse (set by Finlay Wild in 2013) stands at 2 hours, 59 minutes and 22 seconds. Danny MacAskill has even cycled it. But we had been blessed by the mountain gods and we were happy enough just to have experienced the Cuillin's magic.

And what's more, we even came to appreciate Gaelic!

The other members of the expedition were Jane Watts and Mike Pescod.

The author abseiling the In Pin

Mount Vinson

On the seven summits

Air Almaty
ALE

Mount Vinson

16

7Up - an Antarctic Adventure (2015)

Full circle: nearly forty years of adventure from the Arctic to the Antarctic, and the final chapter of my seven summits odyssey…

When I informed my friends that I was going to climb Mt Vinson they usually said "*Where the f*k's that?*"

So I did (wear the fox hat). Well there's nothing like a bit of fur to keep out the cold, is there?

A rather corny gag perhaps, but whilst most people are familiar with Kilimanjaro and Everest, very few have heard of Vinson, let alone recognise that it is Antarctica's highest peak.

Double the size of Australia, Antarctica is our planet's fifth largest continent; an island 'east of the sun, west of the moon and south of everything else'. Its 5.4 million square mile ice cap is so heavy that it pushes the underlying land down below sea level. Antarctica is a place rich in contradictions and paradoxes. It contains the largest body of fresh water on earth (90% of the world's ice and 68% of its fresh water) although its interior is an icy desert, with annual precipitation measured in mere millimetres. Much of it is a featureless plateau and yet overall it has the greatest average elevation of all the continents (1,860m/6,100ft). It is of course the coldest continent, with the lowest recorded temperature on Earth's surface (−93.2°C/ −135.8 °F) but although its average summer temperature is a chilly -20°C (-30°F) the intense 24-hour ultraviolet sunlight is strong enough to melt snow on dark objects (during summer, more solar radiation reaches the surface at the South Pole than is received at the Equator in an equivalent period). For six months of the year the sun never rises and for six months it never sets, for each year it rises only once (in September) and sets only once (in March).

When you think of the frozen continent you probably bring to mind visions of Scott, Shackleton and endless ice; an historic paradigm shaped by tales of epic endeavour and heroic failure. Whilst this imagery is of course part of the continent's rich heritage, in truth the Antarctica of today is a world apart from the vast, empty Terra Incognita of the early 20th century (of that, more anon…). Historic speculation over the existence of a 'southern land' was confirmed in the early 1820s when British, American and Russian expeditions began exploring the Antarctic Peninsula region and other areas south of the Antarctic Circle, but it took until 1840 to establish that Antarctica was indeed a continent and not an archipelago, or a frozen ocean. We know much about the early 20th century explorations, but there was little other human activity there until after World War II, when an upsurge in scientific research led to the establishment of some fifty supporting stations, camps and refuges by several nations. Although some countries (UK included) have made Antarctic territorial claims, these are not universally recognised, and so a Treaty was negotiated in 1959 that neither denies nor recognises these claims. On our planet there are few places indeed where there has never been war, where the environment is fully protected, and where scientific research is a priority, but we can be proud to boast a whole continent like this, called by the Antarctic Treaty '*... a natural reserve, devoted to peace and science*'. For climbers, scientists, explorers and other early 21st century visitors, this place of peace and science is an extraordinary experience: a once-in-a-lifetime privilege that transcends price, challenging your physical, mental and psychological capabilities and in many cases altering your whole outlook on life.

The Chilean town of Punta Arenas - launch pad for many an Antarctic expedition – can justifiably claim to be the southernmost city in the world. It lies hundreds of miles south of Tasmania and New Zealand on the same latitude as the Falkland Islands. Arriving here from the UK winter after ten thousand miles and several flights you begin to appreciate its southerly position when confronted by 24 hour daylight. With an average January temperature around 10°C (and don't forget that this is their *summer*!) you can often experience four seasons in a day here, from T-shirt sunshine to puffy-parka sleet. At the centre of the city's leafy main square close to the legendary Shackleton Bar is a towering statue of Ferdinand Magellan, the famous explorer who reconnoitred Patagonia in the early 1500s. Below Magellan sit two indigenous bronze figures and a local legend has it that those who kiss 'the native's big toe' will receive good luck and safe travels. As I had only purchased a one-way air ticket here I wasn't going to take any chances. Contagion or no contagion I gave the said pedal extremity 'ae fond kiss' and made a wish. Superstitious - me? Well maybe just a bit!

I had spent several years dreaming of visiting Antarctica and reading up about it, but when the dream finally came true it challenged many of my assumptions. Forget the notion of the continent being the preserve of only a few hard-core scientists and climbers: the population engaging in and supporting science or managing and protecting the Antarctic region varies from approximately four thousand four hundred in summer to one thousand one hundred in winter. Statistics kept by the International Association of Antarctica Tour Operators (yes, there is one!) listed thirty seven thousand visitors to Antarctica in 2013/14 (mostly cruise ships, but visits to the interior are growing steadily). I was also gobsmacked to discover that there is a Lonely Planet Guide to Antarctica "*Start your adventure with the only complete travel guide to the Ice, from the popular Antarctic Peninsula to the white expanse of the South Pole…*" Well colour me amazed…

Scientific and climbing groups gathering in 'Punta' are dealt with by Antarctica Logistics and Expeditions and their subsidiary Adventure Network International. Back in 1985, ALE was the first company in the world to offer flights to the interior of Antarctica using a DC4 aircraft and today it is the sole provider of logistical support and safety backup for Mt. Vinson expeditions. All early expeditions to the frozen continent had to cross the Drake Passage by boat (a hazardous journey in itself) but today's visitors cross the Antarctic Circle on a Russian Ilyutian jet. This Russian airline rejoices in the name 'Air Almaty', causing one expedition member to remark that he hoped that The Almighty *was* in charge and that the Ilyutian *wasn't* an illusion.

So my adventure starts in January 2015, when a trepidatious group of polar travellers mounted the rudimentary steps up into the Ilyutian fuselage and immediately found themselves wondering just how safe the flight from Punta Arenas to the ice shelf was going to be. The aircraft could best be described as a windowless workhorse, having been designed to transport vehicles and equipment (and arms perhaps?) into conflict zones (one crew member was reputed to have said that it made a nice change to land somewhere where you weren't being shot at!). One concession to the unnerved was a large screen onto which was projected a map (showing aerial progress) and a camera (showing exactly where one would crash if one did crash). In fact the camera was a great idea (why don't all airlines have one?) since we were able to watch the Chilean greenery slip beneath us, the Antarctic ice shelf appear and - four and a half hours after departure - the Ellsworth Mountain range herald our imminent arrival on the white continent. Our in-flight concerns were not allayed by the rather serious cabin crew though: a bunch of po-faced Russian blokes (no eye candy there then) who handed out earplugs and flashed occasional commands onto the screen. My particular favourite was "*We are going to descend in forty minutes. You have to take your things to be warmly clothed.*" Ah, goody. That would be Antarctica then.

When we touched down at 1,000m (3,300ft) on the immense runway of blue ice (not on skids, but on wheels) I had imagined that we would have to trudge the five kilometres or so to the main camp Union Glacier but in fact we were whisked away in splendid style by four minibuses with balloon tyres and high ground clearance. Although we had entered Earth's only continent with no native human population, and penetrated its empty interior (no animals, no birds, no insects and no vegetation) I was ridiculously pleased on this first Antarctic journey to see a tree growing on the ice (ok it was only a cardboard cut-out Christmas Tree without any tinsel, but at least it was green! A sentimental gesture by a homesick ALE staff member perhaps?)

As we approached the temporary summer settlement at Union Glacier ('U-Gee' as it's fondly called) we could make out lines of clamshell tents set out with geometrical precision, together with two larger dining tents (the *Fram* and the *Terra Nova*), an ablution block and a veritable array of vehicles: skidoos, snowmobiles and skid planes. Having learned that there were great meals and even hot showers at U-Gee we were excited at the prospect of spending a day or two there, but these promised luxuries were denied us for the time being, when ALE staff informed us that flying conditions were ideal for onward flight to Vinson base camp. Perhaps the most amazing of the fifteen flights that I took during the whole trip to Antarctica and back, was this next one: a thirty minute journey in a DC3. OK, the engines had been upgraded to turboprop, the fuselage had been stretched to take more passengers, and it was called a 'Basler' but basically this was still a seventy year old DC3 plane as seen in many adverts for luxury goods (yes the romance of flight still lives on). All the aircraft here - the Basler and two Twin Otters - are operated by Kenn Borek Air - a Canadian company running contract operations in remote wilderness areas including the Arctic and Antarctic (suffice to say that the pilots of these aircraft are a breed apart). Once deposited onto the snow at Vinson Base Camp at 7,020ft (2,140m) our ten member expedition – now nicknamed '*The InVinsonables*' (geddit?) – set about pitching tents and cutting ice blocks as protection against the wind. At -10°C it all seemed a bit chilly to us, but this was only a mild precursor of things to come: it was going to get a whole lot colder later on. For of course we were only six hundred miles from the South Pole and the average temperature here was -20°C (-18°F). Someone with time on their hands had cut out in giant ice letters the word VINSON and mounted it on a plinth, a picturesque foreground to the eponymous lofty peak above and beyond.

Mount Vinson lies in the aptly-named Sentinel range, a high rampart of ice and rock forming the last gasp of the Andean mountain range, once connected to Antarctica and Africa via a tectonic assemblage called Gondwanaland. It was as late as 1966 - nearly two hundred years after James Cook circumnavigated Antarctica - that the summit of Mt. Vinson was first reached, by an American expedition, thus becoming the last of the seven summits to be conquered. The name

Vinson was given in tribute to US Congressman Carl Vinson who was influential in promoting Antarctic exploration. This accident of geography – Antarctica's place of pilgrimage for seven-summiteers - has led to a small but important source of business for ALE and Kenn Borek Air. What sets the mountain apart from the world's other seven summits is not only its intense cold and physical isolation, but also - paradoxically - its unique safety record. For despite the demands it makes on climbers in terms of technical ability and physical fitness, as yet nobody has died climbing it, unlike the other six (Kosciusko included). In part this is because it is often kept back by experienced '7-summiteers' as their grand finale (indeed three of our ten member group were to gain that accolade during this expedition).

Like Denali, but unlike Aconcagua and Everest, there are no Sherpas, porters, mules or horses to transport expedition supplies here. And for ten years there have been no dogs in Antarctica either, since an Environmental Protocol required that all canines be removed because of concerns that they might transfer diseases like distemper to seals, and fears that they could disturb the wildlife. So - in the absence of any assistance - we had to carry all our own stuff along the Branscomb Glacier to Low Camp – an uphill climb of around five miles. This required roping up in teams of four or five (in case of crevasses), carrying our rucksacks and pulling sleds, with anything up to 100lbs weight in total.

My assumption that it would always be cold in Antarctica was rudely shattered on sledge haul day when the wind dropped completely. Reflected in the valley walls, the strong 24-hour ultraviolet light was enough to burn unprotected skin quite quickly. So nose guards, light buffs and plenty of sunscreen were called for on the slow march up to our next temporary home at 2,750 m (9,000ft). Once there it was another case of putting up tents and preparing for the next uphill struggle. Oh, and going to the toilet…

I've often found that armchair expeditioners have a somewhat prurient interest in wilderness toilet protocol (and it doesn't get much more unusual than lavatory etiquette in Antarctica). Peeing is only permitted in designated pee holes (between camps these are few and far between). Unless you want to put on all your cold weather gear and walk over to a pee hole, relieving yourself at night requires the use of a pee bottle, which is fine except that if you don't then keep it in your sleeping bag you end up the next morning with a problematic permanently frozen yellow bottle. And let's just say woe betide you if you mistake your pee bottle for a water bottle...

Now when it comes to solid human waste the picture gets much more complicated. Under the Antarctic Treaty human sewage shall, "to the maximum extent practicable" be removed from the area by the generator of such wastes. What this means in practice is that pooing is confined to special boxes (at lower camps) and so-called Wag Bags (at higher camps). These are plastic bags containing a powder that turns waste into a stable gel. Now lest I stray into the realms of 'too much information' gentle reader, suffice it to say that all solid waste is bagged up, removed and flown back to Chile. This isn't as unpleasant as it sounds, since everything freezes so quickly in Antarctica, but - as one who volunteered to sledge back half of the expedition's solid waste to Base Camp - I can testify that the combined excrement of ten beefy male climbers amounts to a complete load of crap, (and now let's just leave the lavatory humour at that shall we…)

The main physical obstacle for climbers en route to the top of Antarctica is the Headwall – almost a kilometre of ice sloping up to 45° that ascends steeply towards a saddle between Mt Vinson and Mt Shinn (third highest mountain in Antarctica). The presence of fixed ropes on the headwall helped us greatly, enabling steady jumaring[1] on the way up and arm-arresting on the way down. Once at the top of the fixed ropes a gentler slope leads up to High Camp at 3,770 m (12,400ft): a small patch of fairly level ice with stunning views of Shinn. A short walk from here to a rocky cliff top perch ('the edge of the world') revealed tiny specks of our Low Camp tents far below, with stunning mountain ranges beyond that, and in the distance, a vast empty expanse of Antarctic nothingness punctuated by the occasional nunatak[2].

Our slow but steady upward progress was punctuated by periodic rest days and of course we followed the maxim 'climb high, sleep low' by revisiting Low Camp again, so that when we finally approached summit day we were as fit, rested and acclimatised as we could possibly be. Despite all the preparation, when summit day did arrive there were all the usual concerns about the right kit and the right weather, for our radioed forecast suggested temperatures of -28°C and winds gusting up to 30 knots (35 mph) – borderline conditions for a successful attempt. But our legendary guides Vern and Lakpa reassured us that if things became too gnarly we would return to High Camp and try again the next day.

As it was, in the event, the mountain Gods smiled on us. The wind was not as bad as had been forecast for our nine mile, ten hour climb. With Mt Shinn falling ever lower behind us, we gradually ascended the summit valley, pressure breathing every step in the cold, thin air. After several hours we regrouped at the start of the summit ridge to 'layer up' for the steeper ice slopes to come. As we slowly inched our way along the spectacular rocky ridge leading to that small patch of hallowed ground - the top of Antarctica - I knew beyond any doubt that I was going to

---

[1]A technique used to ascend a rope using a hand-held device.

[2]A nunatak (from Inuit nunataq) is an exposed, often rocky element of a ridge, mountain, or peak not covered with ice or snow within an ice field or glacier.

make it. What happened next is difficult to put into words, but basically I found myself letting go, overwhelmed by a massive wave of uncontrollable emotion. This, finally, was the place I had dreamed of seeing for so many years. This, finally, was the end of a twenty year epic adventure that had taken me to the high point of every continent. I was about to become one of only a small number of Brits ever to complete all of the seven summits and as far as I knew only the second (after my friend and inspiration Al Sutcliffe) to have managed this without any failed attempts.

As I stepped up to the top of Antarctica, the true scale, majesty and magnificence of the white continent were overwhelming. On one side the curvature of the earth could be discerned along the distant horizon. On the other side, remote peaks - most never touched by human boots - stretched out below me. I was in heaven - or at least as near to heaven on earth as I was likely to get. It was, finally, the end of an era, the end of an Antarctic Adventure and the end of my Seven Summits odyssey. It was all too much and I started to sob uncontrollably.

This was a big mistake as it froze the inside of my goggles in an instant, obscuring all visibility.

So, I'm going to recommend right here and now: would all climbers completing their seventh summit please keep their emotions in check and refrain from crying.

Yeah, right!

Postscript

Luckily enough, it was only at the relative comfort of U-Gee that we experienced some of the worst weather of the whole expedition. Strong winds chilled the air temperatures significantly and blew spindrift mounds against the tents so that from time to time we had to dig out our escape route. Whilst this delayed our return, it gave us a chance to savour the delights and distractions of U-Gee, like kite skiing, fat tyre biking, games of Scrabble and great food.

But the weirdest coincidence happened during this enforced stopover.

One afternoon, after listening to a lecture on early Antarctic explorers, the bearded figure sitting next to me suddenly turned to me and said in his broad north-eastern voice, "*Hello Jimmy!*" This figure turned out to be none other than Conrad Dickinson, first and only Briton to achieve the polar 'grand slam' (crossing Greenland, the South Pole and the North Pole all unsupported). An experienced polar guide, Conrad had played a leading part in Prince Harry's

'Walking with the Wounded' 2013 Antarctica event. On this occasion he had been leading a private client on a 222km charity trek to the South Pole and had recently flown in to U-Gee.

Having lived round the corner from the family in Hexham, Conrad had shared many training, climbing and cycling sessions with me over a ten year period, but we lost touch when I moved to Scotland. And here he was, larger than life and twice as lively. It is, indeed, a small world. Soon after I returned to the UK I went to see him in his gracious home overlooking Hadrian's Wall.

"*Typical Ogilvie,*" he grinned at me, "*I don't see you for 15 years and then it's twice in 48 hours!*".

During the Vinson climb I shared tent space with John Zeckendorf, a Tasmanian blessed with a British sense of humour. Super-efficient, he was the ideal team mate, always good humoured, supportive and ahead of the curve when it came to pitching and striking camp.

Mount Vinson

Mount Vinson

Toubkal

Afterword

As I'm a glass-half-full, pain-avoider personality I may have given the impression in these pages, of adventures being rather easier than they are. To be sure I haven't dwelt very much upon the physical hardships of 'living on the edge'; the lung-bursting altitude, the cold-induced misery and the general vicissitudes of extreme environments. Neither have I devoted many paragraphs to the irritating, frustrating and sometimes imbecilic behaviour of expedition team members. Believe me, they do exist, and if you like reading about that sort of thing there are plenty of other books out there that cover such difficulties - often in forensic detail. But, unless you are organising an expedition and can therefore choose participants, you just have to try to get on as best as you can with whoever turns up. As time goes by one's initial expectations are sometimes thwarted, with erstwhile kindred spirits turning out to be otherwise - and, happily - vice versa. A coping strategy that I have found works well for me in these 'big brother' household situations is to avoid letting people 'get to you', for example by avoiding taking sides and being drawn into personality conflicts; by teaming up with kindred spirits for tent sharing; and by 'escaping' - reading, listening to music or keeping a diary. In any expedition

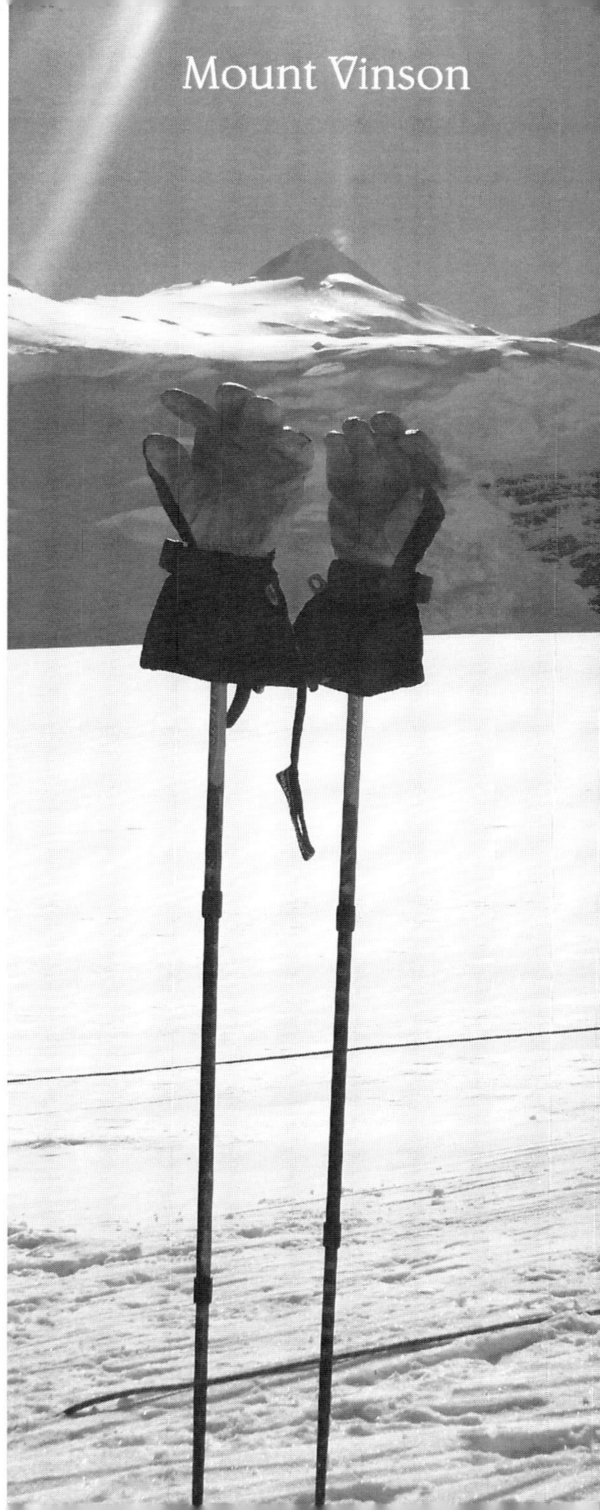

the importance of being 'sorted' psychologically cannot be overestimated: on more than one occasion I have seen otherwise physically and mentally fit people fail because of psychological difficulties.

Looking back on these pages I feel immensely privileged to have been able to pursue such a rich variety of adventures at the same time as being a parent and following a career in forestry. The time has positively flown by and although I'm not a great one for dishing out advice, I do therefore have one exhortation to make, and that is please don't wait. You never know what's around the corner and life is too short and precious to be wasted in prevarication: in the dying days of their lives, most people regret the things they didn't do more than the things they shouldn't have done.

Many happy adventures – and many happy returns!

James Ogilvie 2015

Mount Vinson

Mount Vinson

Rwenzori

Tree Aid… "*without trees we have no life*"

Tree Aid was established as a charity in 1987 by a group of UK foresters responding to the chronic poverty and environmental crisis affecting Africa. It is a uniquely forestry-focused charity which provides funding, training and support to local communities in the worst affected parts of rural Africa.

Trees feed, house, provide energy and improve the environment for millions of families in the Sahel[1]. But rapid deforestation in these African drylands is depriving many people of their basic resources. Tree Aid works village by village, helping communities to unlock the potential of trees and forests and allowing them to meet their basic needs and generate income. Amongst the many activities supported by Tree Aid are:

- Managing natural woodlands sustainably.
- Establishing and managing tree nurseries.
- Growing trees on and around farmland and villages.
- Promoting agro-forestry to improve/conserve agricultural soils so that more food can be grown.
- Developing business planning skills for villagers generating non-timber products such as fruits, oils, honey and medicines.
- Helping village entrepreneurs to organise themselves to gain better access to markets and services.

Each year Tree Aid works with over 350 communities in places like Burkina Faso, Ethiopia, Ghana and Mali. Since it was established, Tree Aid's efforts have ensured that:

- 7.2 million trees have been planted across Africa.
- Hundreds of thousands more trees have naturally regenerated through improvements in

[1]African drylands.

natural resource management .

- Over 450,000 villagers have benefitted from improved incomes from tree products meaning better health, education and life chances .
- Over 1,000,000 people have benefitted from improvements in soil and water conservation.
- The survival rate of trees in communities supported by Tree Aid is 60-70% compared with an average of 40% on other tree planting initiatives.

In thirty years, Tree Aid has grown from a turnover of only fifty thousand pounds to over four million pounds. That means that it is still relatively modest compared to most of the long-established, household-name charities. Nevertheless it is highly effective, punching above its weight in all sorts of ways. Tree Aid's work will continue to transform the lives of thousands of people living in sub-Saharan Africa.

In the words of one farmer on a Tree Aid funded project, 'without trees we have no life'. Tree Aid provides that vital lifeline.

See http://treeaid.org.uk/

Rwenzori

Acknowledgements and thanks

I would like to thank all those individuals and companies who put their faith in me and kindly sponsored me on Everest and Vinson, and in particular:-

Barrell Tree Consultants
Citibank
Forest Carbon Ltd
Howie Forest Products
W. Jenkinson Forest Products
Stuart Milne Group
Network Veka
Norbord (Big thanks to Dave McElroy)
Northern Rock
Novograf (Big thanks to Alistair Miller)
Ogilvie & Company
Scottish Woodlands
Tullis Russell Papermakers Ltd
Hugh Wark

Lakpa Rita and **Vern Tejas** were immensely helpful on Everest and Vinson.

Thanks to **Many Rivers Press** for permission to quote **David Whyte**'s poems and a shout out to **Dire Straits** for permission to quote from Brothers in Arms.

Many thanks to Dorothy and Russell Bruce of Twinlaw Publishing.

The poem by Vera Brittain is reproduced by permission of Mark Bostridge and T.J. Brittain-Catlin, Literary Executors for the Estate of Vera Brittain 1970.

Maps supplied by Pure Communication.

Chris Bonington has been an inspiration and supportive of my endeavours.

A big thanks to the many, many individuals who kindly donated some £50,000 to Tree Aid during my quest for the seven summits. See for example https://www.justgiving.com/jamesogilvie/ and https://www.justgiving.com/james7summits/

But most of all, thanks to my long-suffering parents and to Rachel and Sarah.

Chapter 2 first appeared in the 1983 Journal of the Royal Scottish Forestry Society.
Chapter 8 first appeared online as a 2005 Jagged Globe trip report.
Chapter 9 first appeared in 2007 as a Cowalfest publication.
Chapter 14 first appeared online in 2010 in Scotland Outdoors.
Chapter 13 first appeared online in 2010 in the publication puls polonii.

I promise myself
to the mountain
and to the foundation
from which
my future comes.

From **Pilgrim** by **David Whyte** (printed with permission from Many Rivers Press www.davidwhyte.com)

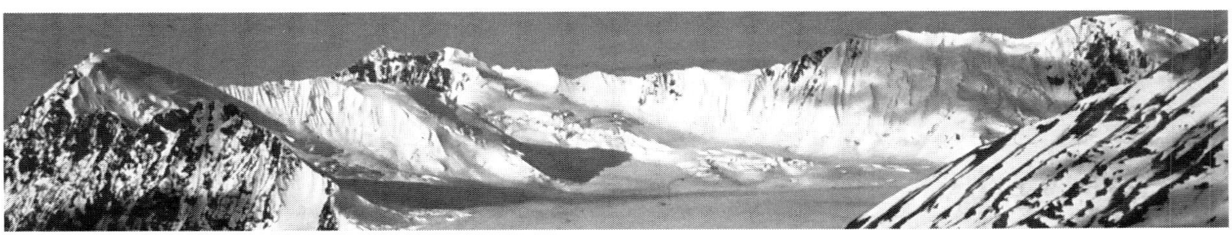

McKinley